2-

D1588550

LETTERS FROM ENGLAND

Letters from England

EÇA DE QUEIROZ

Translated
by Ann Stevens

OHIO UNIVERSITY PRESS

English translation © The Bodley Head 1970
Printed by offset and bound in the
United States of America for
Ohio University Press, Athens, Ohio
by Cushing-Malloy, Ann Arbor, Mich.
LC 70-123109
ISBN 8214-0080-0

Contents

Translator's Preface

Letters from England, written in their original form for the Rio de Janeiro *Gazeta de Notícias*, were begun in 1879 while Eça de Queiroz, then in his late thirties, was Consul in Newcastle-upon-Tyne and financial difficulties were impeding his transfer to Bristol. The following years mark Eça's maturity as a writer, and in the letters, as in his fiction, we see the novelist's imagination working together with a keen observation. If all the details in the following letters are not strictly correct, this does not mar the keenness of his appreciation of the contemporary political and social situation. We know it was the 92nd Regiment of the Line that was defeated by the Boers and not the 94th (p. 31); Santa Claus and Father Christmas are not two distinct persons (p. 34); the Three Wise Men came from Gotham and not Chester (p. 40). Also, Disraeli died on 19th April, not 19th May (p. 81) and was M.P. for Maidstone, not for Wycombe (p. 92), and the quotation from *Tancred* (p. 87) is not accurate—but these errors do not detract from his vivid picture of the late Prime Minister. Similarly, if his extracts from the two articles in the *Times* on Brazil and Portugal (pp. 166 ff.) are not wholly faithful, we must remember that he was writing for Brazilian readers and seeking to entertain them. In the final letter, the 'practical joke' has been substantially embroidered upon to provide the reader with the maximum amusement: the 'ten or twelve lines' which Eça claimed were taken out and replaced by others were

7

in fact no more than one 'gross line maliciously inter-polated in a few copies only of the issue', as the newspaper explained. The speech, furthermore, was published neither on the fourth nor on the fifth but on the seventh page. The letters taken together, however, are an amusing, satirical account of some aspects of Victorian life.

On Books

OCTOBER HAS ARRIVED, and with this month of falling leaves, new books begin to appear—whose leaves are often as ephemeral as those on the trees, but without their pleasing colour and rustle and shade.

We are, in fact, at the height of the Book Season.

These two months, September and October, embrace the most interesting, the most fertile Seasons of English life and they deserve to, for their light and colour and tranquillity make them the best in all the year.

The celebrated London Season, when the Aristocracy, upper and lower, the *top ten thousand* as they used to say, the *cream*, as they say now, return from their country parks and palaces to their mansions and gardens in London, takes place in April, June and July. But this is a vain idle Season of fashions and gloved lackeys, champagne, gambling and cotillons. While the other Seasons! . . .

Consider the useful, dynamic solemn Seasons that abound in these golden months of September and October. They are more like it! We have, for instance, the Congress Season.

What a spectacle that produces! All the green surface of England, from North to South, is then dotted with black patches. They are congresses in the course of deliberation. There are metaphysical ones and culinary ones.

Here some surly discontented individuals elaborate a new social order; over there a crowd of wise men crouch for weeks on end around a dark object, unable to decide whether it is a recent worthless slab or a flagstone from the nuptial chamber of Queen Guinevere; and further on a greasy, shiny group of gentlemen agree upon the fattening power of the sucking-pig—that delicious creature!—as though they were propounding a doctrinal definition.

The most notable congresses this year were the Congress of Medicine in London, attended by one thousand three hundred people, doctors and surgeons from both worlds and both sexes, which promised humanity the suppression of epidemics by vaccines in a few years' time; the British Association, the great Society of Sciences (an annual conference held this year in York) at which the President, Sir John Lubbock, a charming and learned man who has spent his lifetime studying the lower civilizations of insects, laborious democracies of ants, deplorable oligarchies of bees, was this time concerned, as he conducted a survey of science over the last fifty years, with describing some of the stupendous skills of that other ephemeral insect—man. Finally there was an annual Church Conference at Newcastle, composed of bishops, ecclesiastical dignitaries, theologians, doctors of divinity, this extensive Anglican clergy, which is the most learned and literary of all Europe. Here the *Influence of Art in Religious Life and Thought* was discussed, among other subjects: but, as far as I am concerned, the most striking fact was the incidental mention that church attendance decreases by a third every decade, while the religious spirit increases in the masses, so that religious sentiment daily becomes further detached from the decrepit and perishable religious forms.

At this moment there are other congresses—the metallurgical one, the Social Sciences one, the Telegraphists', the Archeological, the Engravers', and so on. . . . Hundreds in fact. Even the Browningites. Do you not know what the Browningites are? A vast association whose aim is to study, comment upon, interpret, venerate, propagate, illustrate and deify the works of the poet Browning. This, even in this country of passionate intellectual enthusiasms, seems to me somewhat exaggerated. Browning is undoubtedly, together with Shelley, Shakespeare and Milton, one of the four leading masters of English poetry: but he has the disadvantage of still being alive. He himself, in person, with jacket and umbrella, attends the congress of which he is the spiritual object and the subject: and his being present fatally tends to turn literary admiration into idolatry, and his hand-shakes naturally become more appreciated in the congress than the poems he wrote. Thus this very deification reduces his stature: he is no longer the great poet of England but becomes the particular idol of the Browningites; he is no longer a spirit communicating with other spirits but an idol dominating the hearts of the superstitious.

But to continue with the Seasons, we still have the Yachting Season, the season of regattas and yachting trips. In England today the possession of a yacht is the same as the possession of a carriage is for us—the first social duty of the established or newly rich, one of the most trivial forms of luxury. A yacht is not necessarily a fragile and graceful boat of some fifty tons and white sails; it can also be a powerful black ship run by steam, weighing two thousand tons and with a crew of sixty. In the latter case, instead of sailing idly round the flowers and lawns of the Isle of Wight, or dipping into the prodigious seascapes off the north coast of Scotland, it cruises round the world, loaded with Bibles for the little Patagonians and with love and champagne for the pretty missionaries aboard her dressed in sailor outfits. Life aboard a yacht has its special customs, its etiquette, its phraseology, its own morals, and above all its own literature. The literature on yachting is enormous—William Black, author of *White Sails*, of *Sunrise*, and *Princess of Thule* is its official novelist; he is a marvellous landscape painter, incidentally, and has in his pen all the vigour that Jules Breton carried in his brush.

Then we have the Shooting Season this month, which opens on September 1st with all the solemnity and public excitement which must, I imagine, have marked the eve of the Great Revolution when the States-General was summoned. I must beg pardon for this abominable comparison—but the flesh is weak and I consider this season sublime. It is at this time that grouse is shot, at this time that grouse is eaten. You do not know what grouse is? It is a bird the size of a partridge, that lives (God bless it!) on the moors of Scotland. Now let me rest for a moment and linger awhile in quiet ecstasy, thinking about grouse with my hands crossed upon my stomach, a tender smile lighting up my eyes as I lick my lips . . . You cannot imagine how greedy I am! But one should never talk of good things without the proper reverence. Lord Beaconsfield, that master of fine living, gave us an example when he mentioned in one of his books the ortolan, that other delicious bird, and added that the ortolan's breast is more delightful than a woman's, its aroma more perturbing than lilacs and the flavour of its meat finer than the taste of truth. One might say the same of grouse.

To continue, we also have the Burglary Season—the season when houses are burgled. This also begins in September when the rich depart from London and leave their mansions either shut up or in the care of an old sleepy caretaker. The London burglars, a social body as well-organized as the police itself, then proceed systematically, using disciplined teams and the most perfect scientific methods, to enter and steal from these properties crammed with fine things.

Then we have the Lecture Season. Its name is sufficient explanation and it would take a long time to go into the details of its organization. Let it suffice to say that during this season there is perhaps not one district in London (one could almost say not one street) nor village in the rest of the country, where an individual cannot be seen, every night, with his glass of water before him, expounding upon some subject or other, before a compact, attentive audience conscientiously taking notes. The subjects are of the most varied, from the idea of God to the best way of manufacturing shoe-polish. And the lectures include everybody, from Professor Huxley to some gentleman or other, Mr So-and-so, who steps on to the platform and recounts his impression of a journey to the Fiji Islands, or curious capacities he has observed in his dog . . .

There are yet other Seasons which need not be desscribed: the Hunting Season (fox-hunting that is, which is a world in itself); the Cricket Season: twelve gentlemen who have come from the depths of Australia, and another twelve from the Highlands of Scotland, meet in London to play a tremendous match which lasts three days before a deliriously excited audience.

We also have the Angling Season, angling being that most noble institution to which we are indebted for salmon and trout. It is the favourite sport of the cultured upper middle class, of magistrates and men of learning and that part of the old aristocracy upon which fall the responsibilities of the State. All this world of solemn respectability and high ceremonial goes angling. Perhaps that is why, of all English sports, angling is one of those which have produced the most considerable literature— so considerable that its bibliography, the simple enumeration of its treatises, occupies a book two hundred pages long! Here I respectfully observe the mention of a ponderous study on *Angling among the Assyrians*!

Only this week literature on angling gave us two new books, according to the lists: *An Angler's Notebook* and *Along the River Banks*.

There is then the Travelling Season, when the famous British tourist makes his appearance on the Continent. At this period (September and October) every self-respecting Englishman (or one who, not being able in his deepest conscience to be self-respecting, at least pretends that his neighbour respects him) gets a good dozen

14

trunks ready and sets off for the sunny countries, for the lands of wine and gaiety. The angels (if they did not dream it, as John of God says) must surely, from their blue terrace on high, participate in an amusing spectacle: all England huddled together at the port of Dover, and from there swarms of tourists successively set out—little black lines stretching all over the Continent, spreading to the valley of the Rhine, blackening the snow of the Alps, winding their way through the fruit-groves of Andalucia, flocking into Italian cities and inundating France! All these are English. All these carry a guide-book under their arm. All these take notes. He might travel with his wife, a sister-in-law, a friend of the sister-in-law, an acquaintance of this friend, seven children, six servants, ten dogs and other dog acquaintances of these dogs; and he pays for everything without a murmur! No, this is not true, he grumbles all the time. The Englishman spends most of his pleasure-trip cursing (to himself, for neither the Bible nor his respectability allows him to curse aloud).

The fact is that the Englishman does not enjoy himself on the Continent: he does not understand foreign languages; he finds the food strange; everything which is foreign—customs, clothes, ways of thinking—everything shocks him; he suspects that he is being robbed; he has the vague belief that the bed-linen in the hotels is never clean; seeing theatres open on a Sunday and the crowds amusing themselves brings bitterness to his Christian and puritanical soul; he does not dare to open a foreign book because he suspects he will find obscenities within; if his guide-book states that there are six columns in such

and such a cathedral and he finds only five he feels unhappy for a week and furious with the country he is in,
like a man who has been robbed of a column; and if he
loses a cane, or the train is not on time, he will shut himself in his hotel for a whole day to compose a letter to the
Times, in which he accuses continental countries of being
in an absolutely savage state and sunk in the depths of a
putrid demoralization. The Englishman is an unhappy
creature abroad. Naturally I am not speaking here of the
numerous travellers of taste and literary and artistic
talent: I am speaking of the flocks of middle-class and
tradespeople. But even these latter find their labour as
tourists is compensated when they return to England and
can tell their friends how they were here and there and
they climbed Mont Blanc, and dined at a hotel in Rome,
and, what the deuce!, he and the girls made the devil of a
sensation! ...

What other Seasons are there? The Speech Season,
when, during the Parliamentary vacation, all the politicians spread over the country and discourse at enormous
meetings upon matters of public interest. It is one
of the most curious characteristics of political life in
England.

There are many other Seasons in September and
October, but I cannot recall more at the moment. And
to be fair, I should also mention the Season of autumn.

*

Of all these I naturally find the Book Season the most
interesting.

This does not mean that no books are published outside this season (October to March) in England. Far from it, thank Heaven! Similarly it does not mean that there is no dancing outside the London Season or no travel outside the Travelling Season. It merely means that the large publishers in London and Edinburgh reserve their sensations for launching during this season. A book by Darwin, a study by Matthew Arnold, a poem by Tennyson, a novel by George Meredith, would obviously be held for the Season. Not that this phenomenal amount of printed matter suffers any interruption throughout the year; this vast, loud spate of books spreads out, gradually superimposing upon the crust of the earth another crust of paper printed in the English language.

I do not know if it is possible to calculate the number of volumes published annually in England. I should not be surprised if it went into tens of thousands. I have in front of me yesterday's issue of the *Spectator* with the list of books published this week: *ninety-three works*! And this is merely the *Spectator*'s list; merely what is here called *general literature*. This does not include reprints, nor editions of the classics in all their various formats, from the folio which only a Hercules could lift, to the miniature volume the print of which needs a microscope to read, and in prices ranging from £50 to a few pence. Nor does this include translations of foreign books, especially of ancient literature: nor, finally, does it include the ceaseless flow of books from the Universities—classics, commentaries and glossaries, and folios which spill out of the Clarendon Press by the crate-load.

There is amid this general literature a type of which the

Englishman never tires—travel literature. I am not talking now of novels: this can no longer be considered literary production but rather industrial manufacture. In English domestic life the novel has become an object of prime importance, like flannel or cotton; and so a population of novelists is employed in manufacturing this article, wholesale, and as quickly as the pen can write, flinging the scarcely dry pages on to the market in their anxious desire to beat their rivals.

But the appetite for travel books is also considerable, and scarcely surprising in a foot-loose and expansionist race, with fleets in every sea, colonies in every continent, administrators on every beach, missionaries among every sort of savage, and in the depths of his soul the eternal dream, the beloved dream to remake the Roman Empire. This has produced another sort of literary industrialist— the travel-writer.

In former days a journey was recounted if one happened to have had an interesting trip: the man who had visited distant lands and had enjoyed picturesque adventures, took up his pen when he returned and sat beside his fire; he relived those days, happily recounting his impressions and the scenery he had passed through. But not today. Today the journey is undertaken purely to write the book. A map is opened, a wild exotic spot on the universe is selected, and off the traveller sets with a ream of paper and a dictionary. And the whole point, (as there is considerable competition) is to discover a corner of the earth about which no book has yet been written! Or, when a country is already tolerably well-known, to see if there is still not some little village, some out-of-the-way little river, which might produce three hundred or so pages of prose . . .

Nowadays when one discovers in some odd spot on the globe an individual wearing a sun-helmet, with a pair of binoculars around his neck and a pencil in his hand, don't think this is an explorer, a missionary, a learned botanist collecting rare flowers—it is merely an English writer preparing his next volume.

To illustrate, there is nothing like an example. Here is the list of travel-books published in London *this last fortnight*.

Naturally I have not read them, nor even set eyes on them. I shall merely copy out the titles from the lists of two literary journals: the *Atheneum* and the *Academy*. Note that these books are in general written with care, the descriptions are vivid, the landscape is portrayed with all its colour and light, the city with its movement and its characteristics; they are clear and they are critical; they are observant and geographically correct; and they all generally succeed in capturing the life of the people visited, in every characteristic detail in their daily round, their religion and agriculture and sport and vices, and art if they have any. This is a literature, then, of appreciable importance: a shrewd, patient, meticulous inquiry into every part of the universe.

Here, then, is the list of books published this last fortnight: *My Journey to Medina—Among Han's Sons—In Salt Waters—Far Away in the Pampas—Sanctuaries of Piedmont—The New Japan—A Visit to Abyssinia—Life in the West of India—Up the Mahakam and Down the Barita —On Horseback Through Asia Minor—Scenes of Ceylon—*

Through Towns and Fields—In My Bungalow—Matabele Lands—Flight to the South—Lands of the Midnight Sun— Pilgrimages in Patagonia—Egyptian Sudan—Land of the Magyars—Through Siberia—Notes on the Western World —Routes Through Palestine—Norsk, Lapp and Finn— Wars, Pilgrimages and Waves—Lovely Athens—The White Sea Peninsula—Men and Events of India—On board the 'Fox'—Sport in the Crimea and the Caucasus— Nine Years' Hunting in Africa—Diary of an Idle Man in Sicily—East of Jordan . . .

There are others, many others—and all in a fortnight!

It would be interesting to give a parallel list of poems, books of poetry and odes, ballads, tragedies, advertised or already published in the first fortnight of the season; but I have not the patience to go into all this lyricism. There is a 'great sensation': the book of Dante Rossetti, one of the modern masters: the rest is merely a gentle, sad little group of nightingales.

No less lengthy are the lists of books on theology, controversy, exegesis, etc., which seem to exude the melancholy air of a cemetery. There is the customary assortment in metaphysics—thick and vague, as Herbert Spencer would say. In history, biography, criticism, the bibliographical lists are extravagantly rich . . . All in all it seems to be a magnificent book season. I do not mention novels: heaps of them, hills of them—dung-hills at times!

A rustic shepherdess from the Ardennes, who had never seen any sight more pleasing to her heart than the goats she guarded, was once taken from her hills to Paris, when a regiment went marching along the boulevard, their tricolour fluttering in the breeze. The maiden went white as a sheet and could only mutter at this moment of beatitude:

'Jesus! Look at all those men!'

I do not know whether I am repeating the ridiculous attitude of this shepherdess when I gasp, open-mouthed, as if I had also just arrived from the Ardennes: 'Jesus! Look at all those books!'

But is not this cry as natural as the shepherdess's?

The bedouin from the western desert, when he crosses the Libyan Plateau and sees for the first time the slow, immense Nile filling the valley, cries out in wonder:

'Allah! Look at all that water!'

Water is his great preoccupation: all the sorrows of the sands he inhabits come from their lack of water: more than anyone he appreciates the marvels of this element, and in his cry there is a timid rebuke towards Allah: 'So much water here, and so little from where I come . . .'

And from where I come . . . But let the astute reader complete the comparison for himself.

Winter in London

EVERY DAY I MEET HIM and even at this very moment I can hear him out there in the street, in the gloomy fog of late October, with his plaintive, muted voice: it is not the demi-god of legend with his snow-flake beard and his snow-white mantle, blowing on his fingers as he carries the classic bundle of wood: it is a sooty youth with an old cap and a whip in his hand, who drives a black cart with a hefty *percheron* in the shafts along the frost-hardened macadam, and calls out from door to door his melancholy cry: 'Coals! Coals!'

The beautiful English autumn has therefore drawn to a close! There is nothing to match the gentle soothing charm of mid-October in these southern counties. An afternoon walk along the picturesque banks of the Severn, or beside the Avon, a river which Shakespeare's memory has made almost sacred, or over the lovely Surrey hills, is the most beautiful, most useful sort of relaxation that the spirit can enjoy, exhausted by books and by the wearing bustle of life.

There is something here of that ethereal peace of which the pagan poets dreamed in their ineffable glimpses of Elysium: only the particular nature of the North, the Saxon lines of its architecture, the lay-out of the fields, afford the romantic and elegiac note which is missing in the Latin landscape.

One walks in a soft light, in a melancholy golden haze, in an almost painfully tender air: the green of the endless lawns one treads, the restful sleepy lawns under the spreading branches of the ancient aristocratic trees that stand solemn and isolated and immobile in religious withdrawal, leads the soul insensibly towards something very pure; there is a silence of extreme limpidity, like that which must reign beyond the clouds, a silence that does not exist in hot climates, where the incessant rising of sap seems to make a vague murmur, a silence which rests upon the spirit like a caress. And at every moment delightful scenes appear in the distance—a vaporous blue with an ivy-covered tower of some abbey which emerges from amid a cluster of oaks, or a stately avenue through a park where one can glimpse light dresses trailing over the lawns; the historic architecture of a castle, perhaps, with a feudal flag upon a tower, which suddenly appears upon a rise with its terraces of dark marble, or the wide meadows where fine animals are feeding or resting, while a shining river meanders through the green fields and the plaintive sound of a horn calls from the depths of the woods.

In a few days' time, however, there will be only gloomy fog enshrouding hill and vale for months on end, or snow swirling in the wind.

This monotony, which begins to darken the countryside from November onwards, is to be the cause this year of an excellent innovation in the social customs of England. There is to be a Winter Season in London from December to May.

As you know, London is only inhabited from the beginning of May until the first hot days of August. The rest of the year, London is like the fallen Palmira or the gloomy plain of the Petreian Desert. Some three or four million individuals do remain there, it is true: but they are very inferior individuals, made of common clay, and of no social value in England: it is that part of humanity which has no castles nor parks three leagues' long, nor luxurious yachts in which to cruise around the coasts of Scotland, nor does their name feature in the Book of Gold; it is that section of humanity which has none of the famous Norman blood in its veins, that envied blood more precious than Christ's, its praises sung by all the court poets, the blood which was imported by the rough fellows clad in iron and hairy as beasts who accompanied William of Normandy to these islands; it is that part of humanity which Charles Stuart, Charlie the Darling, called the *canaille*, and which the high priest of *La Belle Hélène*—poor Offenbach—dubbed the low masses: it comprises the worker, the artisan, the artist, the teacher, the philosopher, the labourer, the novelist—anyone who thinks, creates and produces.

This is the worthless mob which remains in London: only that superior element of humanity, the ten thousand at the top, as they so picturesquely put it here, leave for their castles, their seaside villas, or their yachts. London, inhabited only by this abject horde, then becomes something like our wretched Cacilhas. No self-respecting gentleman who wishes to keep his good social name would dare confess that he was in London in January: he would risk being thought a shop-keeper, or worse still, a philosopher or poet or some such low fellow, one of the rabble in fact, who have no castle or pack of hounds, and whom no lady would want as a guest.

If a gentleman has urgent business in London and is forced to return to this plebeian desert, then he maintains a strict incognito; perhaps he will not go so far as to arrange false whiskers, but he will not venture into the street except seated in the shady depths of a *coupé* with the blinds pulled down. And with his coat collar concealing his face. But very few would dare so rash an adventure!

But now all of this is to change. This year it will be fashionable to walk up and down Piccadilly or blossom out with a rose in one's buttonhole in Pall Mall in mid-January, enshrouded by fog. So considerable a revolution was, like all successful revolutions, plotted, proclaimed and popularized by women.

For many years now these angels have impatiently been suffering the melancholy of life in the country during the long Saxon winter. At the beginning, after leaving London and the splendours of the Season, their existence was still tolerable. There were elegant regattas at Cowes; they would spend a week on the Isle of Wight; then there would be the parties to celebrate the opening of the hunting season; the yachting season would follow and trips to the coasts of Norway and the Hebrides and the elegant beaches of Normandy; then, when the Court was in Scotland, there was stag-hunting and parties in the evenings. One could still live a bit.

But when December arrived and the snow, Fashion, that dreadful force, obliged the *top ten thousand* to withdraw to their castles and the solitude of the country.

And this was the beginning of the ladies' awful tedium.

When one does not possess a castle and park like those that exist in England, it may seem like a dream of paradise to live in one of these magnificent residences, among artistic masterpieces that have been accumulating through generations, and suites of furniture worth two hundred *contos*, a staff of seventy servants, twenty horses in the stables and a romantic park to walk through in the firm snow under a brilliantly blue sky. But the unfortunate lady, accustomed to such splendours from tne time of her first tooth, no longer finds any charm in them; a simple drive in an old London hansom-cab, stopping at various shops, is infinitely more attractive to her.

Furthermore, life in a castle is grey and empty and miserable. The men, from early in the morning, have their hunting; furious, league-consuming gallops, leaping over hedges after a terrified fox, to the barbaric cry of Tally-ho! Then at night, after a bath and donning evening dress, a strong grog awaits them in the smoking-room. But the unfortunate ladies? They all enjoy grog, but few of them go hunting. Their day is utterly gloomy. A lady of the middle-class in England always has an occupation, even in the richest of families: she embroiders or paints porcelain or makes shirts for the little Patagonians, teaches the housekeeper's children to read, writes her memoirs or corresponds with some theologian on difficult points of doctrine. But a lady of the *ten thousand* does nothing; her great talents—her *toilette*, her skills as a hostess, her political plotting, her brilliance as a conversationalist, her aesthetic chic—qualities in which she shines, have no place in the relative isolation of the castle, beneath torrents of rain. Her natural habitat is a London *salon*. Out in the country, in the long galleries where the banners hang which her ancestors took at Agincourt or Poitiers—or if her worthy ancestors never invaded France, the banners bought in the antique shop round the corner—my Lady yawns; or stretched out on a sofa, in her white Genoese lace negligée, with a novel in her lap, she watches the snow flakes powdering the great oaks in the park.

Then night falls. That is worse. The men who have gallopped some five leagues after foxes, or have been practising some athletic exercise, are tired. With a gardenia in their lapel and a black pearl on their shirt-front, they lie back on the sofa, worn out, lulled half asleep by one of Chopin's nocturnes which a golden-haired angel is playing at the end of the drawing-room; for all the use they are at a flirtation, an amorous intrigue or a cultured conversation they might as well be stuffed with straw.

In vain might the poor ladies spend two hundred pounds on their *toilette*: in vain might their divine shoulders gleam in the candle-light. Nothing has any effect. The gentleman longs to leave the room, enjoy a brandy and soda, and stretch those limbs which the fox has tired, in well-perfumed and well-warmed sheets—and snore at ease.

This situation was intolerable.

And even the men suffered. To gallop over the crisp snow on an excellent horse after the barking pack in the chill morning air has a certain charm. But can this compare with the delight of going along to the club for a gossip and having three or four balls every night and giving one's opinion on the Eastern question and having supper with Miss Fanny in a warm velvet-lined *boudoir*, while outside the plebs splashes along in the London mud? No, there is no comparison.

So the psychological moment arrived, as that worthy master of prose, Mr Bismarck, describes it, when both lords and ladies agreed that winter in the country was good for the wolves, but for the peers of England, London was preferable. So that is how this most unexpected occurrence in English life—winter in London—came about.

And yet winter in London is by no means agreeable, heaven knows! One wakes in the morning to find a thick, grey, chilling shadow enshrouding everything outside the window; one must shave by gas-light and take breakfast with all the candles of the candelabra alight; and the carriage which transports us is preceded by a torch. By midday this scene changes; the shadow loses some of its greyness and by slow odious stages changes to ochre yellow and begins to exude a malodorous vapour. Breathing becomes difficult, one's clothes feel clammy against the skin; the buildings that surround us have the vague, ghostly lines of the cursed cities of the Apocalypse, and the thunder of London's streets, that tumultuous din which must disturb the court of Heaven, becomes a low rumble like a noise echoing from under the ground.

Then at night comes another change: all this shadowiness, this thick clinging, slimy fog turns into rain ... Into rain, did I say? Into mud, liquid mud which slips and drips and comes dribbling out of a black sky.

The gas-light acquires a bloody hue; as everyone drinks heavily and incessantly to combat this freezing, fatal fog, there is a vague smell of alcohol in the streets, which is exuded upon the breath: this excites and urges on the rabble to vicious practices. The intolerable noise of the streets, the bustle of the violent crowds, the brightness of the shop-windows, make the blood race and the nerves vibrate almost painfully; one thinks with intensity and makes one's way impetuously; one's desires are felt intensely; the human beast becomes inflamed: it wants something strong, animal-like, fighting, excess, greed, the flush brandy gives, passion. London exhales violence and crime on a winter's night. And one can be sure that in every one of the carriages which rush by in their thousands, each one with a ruddy glow of its lanterns, some citizen, male or female, sits committing or preparing to commit, with the exception of sloth, one of the Seven Deadly Sins.

Of one thing we can be sure: those who decide to winter in London will not lack topics to chat about: apart from the new books and the scandals which will obviously occur, and the fashions that are always being invented, politics in itself is a never-ending source of discussion: a revolt is certain in Ireland; the leaders of the Land League, members for Ireland, are to be tried for high treason; a new war in Afghanistan, where there has been an uprising in Kabul; all South Africa rebelling; ominous complications from the East; acute differences of opinion between the radicals in power ... A charming state of affairs altogether!

It was in identical circumstances that Granville, the one who wrote the famous *Memoirs*, looked around at all sides of the political and social horizon one early spring, and seeing nothing (in 1830) but black omens of revolt and war and crises and danger for his country, jubilantly, almost ecstatically exclaimed:

'Good Lord! What nights we are going to have at the Club!'

Christmas

CHRISTMAS, THAT GREAT domestic celebration in
England, was sad this year—it had about it that particular sadness one feels on a blazing hot day in the
deserted square of a poor village, the melancholy which
pervades the empty chairs around a dead fire in a room to
which one will never return.

What spoilt Christmas was not the political problems,
dark and stormy though they were; not the rebellion in
the Transvaal, where the Boers began by wiping out the
94th regiment of the Line, one of the most glorious and
experienced regiments of England, and threaten to stir
up a bloody racial war in South Africa; not even the
situation in Ireland, which is no longer governed by
England but by the revolutionary committee of the Land
League—none of this would be sufficient cause for
anxiety to spoil the traditional flavour of their Christmas
Pudding. Public misfortunes have never spoilt the
citizens' appetite: and the country's troubles, so long as
they are not tangible, and take the inescapable form of
howitzers bursting upon a besieged city, will never make
a patriot lose his sleep.

No; what spoilt Christmas was simply the lack of snow.
A Christmas like we have just had, with a sun the pallor of
convalescence, creeping timidly across a vast strip of

31

faded blue silk, a snowless Christmas, a fur-coat-less Christmas, is as insipid and disheartening as St John's Night would be in Portugal—a night of bonfires and serenading—if there were a foot of snow lying on the ground and it hailed until dawn! A national disappointment!

In order to understand the importance of snow in our famous English Christmas better, one needs only look at some of the pictures, engravings or lithographs, which have made it so popular!

In scene after scene the subject never varies: there is always an entrance to a park with a feudal air, and it is Christmas Eve, before midnight; the sky, heavy with impending snow, looks like dirty gauze: and as far as the eye can see everything is covered with fallen snow, a soft, thick, white snow that imposes a great silence upon the countryside. At the park railings a woman and two children stand huddled in their rags holding lanterns in their hands and singing carols; and in the background, amid denuded trees, rise the solid walls of a castle, its windows a-glow, gleaming with the brightness within and the gaiety of those that live there.

And it is in these windows that shine forth upon the snowy night that all the poetry of Christmas lies.

Happy are those for whom these difficult doors open! In the entrance hall one is greeted by the sight of ceilings and doorways and chair-backs and hunting trophies all decorated with Christmas greenery, sacred branches of holly; and on the walls the traditional refrain: *Merry Christmas*! stands out in gilt letters and the same exclamation is repeated when the host shakes hands with his guest.

In the fireplace a huge Christmas fire dances and crackles: its rich glow makes fair hair gleam like gold and white whiskers like silver.

Everything is decorated as if for a sacred Easter celebration: portraits of ancestors are adorned by winter flowers, snow flowers, and all the silver in the house sparkles with patriarchal splendour upon the sideboards. From the beautiful chandeliers hangs the branch of mistletoe, symbolic of domestic love: and woe betide the ladies who delay a moment beneath its leaves and berries! Whoever surprises them has the right to a passionate kiss! What crafty detours, what complicated strategies, to avoid the fatal branch! But poor darlings! either they make a mistake or take fright, and little screams ring out from beneath the mistletoe all the time, and there is a kiss and two arms clasping a fugitive waist. . . .

The piano is never silent these nights! It is an old English ballad which tells of tourneys and knights, or else a Scottish reel, which one dances with all the delightful ceremonial of the past.

And through corridors and drawing-rooms little children dressed in pink and white and their hair flying, run and sing and laugh and keep rushing to look at the hands of the monumental clock, because Santa Claus arrives at midnight; worthy Santa Claus who is three thousand years old and has the softest of hearts, and who at this time of the night is making his way through the snow on the highway, with his pockets full of toys, smiling to himself and leaning on his stick. Dear Santa Claus! To leave the cotton-wool cabin that he inhabits in the Land of Legend at such a cold season and at his advanced age, to come over seas and through forests to bring these babies their Christmas!

And how they adore him! No sooner does he arrive than they all run triumphantly and drag him to the fireside and rub his old frozen hands and offer him a silver goblet full of mead—which he drinks at one gulp, the glutton! Then they dive into his pockets! What delights are there!

But of all the characters that appear at Christmastide, Father Christmas is my favourite.

Father Christmas can only be admired in all his glory when one opens the room where supper is laid: there he is on his pedestal in the centre of the table, reflecting the gleaming crystal and silver. Welcome Father Christmas! Good evening Father Christmas!

The worthy old gentleman, with his snow-spattered hood down to his eyes, his hands hidden in the wide sleeves and a roguish gleam in his eye, spreads his lips in a smile of supreme happiness, and his long cotton-wool whiskers hang to his feet. All the children want to hug him and he does not resist for he is an indulgent old man.

And the gayer the supper grows, the wider spreads his patriarchal smile; his cheeks glow scarlet, and his beard seems to grow even longer. There he is, good-natured and venerable, with all the importance of a well-loved, guardian god, like the sacramental incarnation of domestic happiness.

Yet outside in the snow the poor children sing carols: and how lustily they sing! They know they will not be forgotten: and in a little while the gate will be opened and a servant will come bowed beneath the weight of all sorts of good things—joints of meat and pasties and wine and cheese, even toys for the little ones. Santa Claus is a democrat and if he fills his pockets for the rich it gives him special pleasure to see them emptied in the lap of the poor.

All this is very charming. But take away the snow and everything is spoilt. Christmas with a butter-coloured moon shining upon a tepid, spring-like earth, becomes merely another day on the calendar. There is no intimate poetry in the fire; there are no carols; Santa Claus does not come, Father Christmas looks only like an insipid toy; the mistletoe is not gathered. There is not even the joy of opening the window and setting a dishful of Christmas crumbs on the sill for the sparrows and the other little birds that suffer so in snowy weather. There is no Christmas in fact! That is what happened this year.

There is only the consolation, that the poor were not so cold. And this is the essential point: considering the matter carefully, if there was a little more comfort in lowly cottages and if their inhabitants did not shiver with cold all night under their meagre rags, then it is a matter of indifference that the ladies yawned in their castles.

I do not really know how the sumptuous supper can taste good nor the drawing-room fire manage to bring warmth, when one considers that outside there are people freezing and gnawing a crust of stale bread in some dismal corner. It is precisely at these times of family celebrations that there is a moment's pause in the mad gallop of our selfishness and the soul is open to the better sentiments of fraternity and universal love, and the consciousness of the misery in which so many thousands of creatures struggle returns to us with greater bitterness. At such a time one has only to see a poor little girl standing agape before a shop window, with tears in her eyes for a twopenny doll that she will never hold in her deprived arms—to reach the simple conclusion that this is an abominable world. This feeling gives rise to a few acts of charity at Christmas, but with the holiday over selfishness is given its head again, no one gives another thought to the poor, except a few hardened revolutionaries who deserve to be flung into prison—and poverty continues to sob in its corner.

The philosophers declare that this must always be so: the noblest of them, Jesus, whose very birth we are celebrating, warned us, in an immortal phrase, that 'ye have the poor always with you'. Various revolutions have attempted to prove this sinister prophesy false, but the revolutions pass and the poor are still there.

At this moment, for example, in Ireland, the workers, or rather the serfs of the Duke of Leicester, are dying of hunger, and the Duke of Leicester is drawing, from their excessive labours, an annual four hundred *contos*' income! It is true that Ireland is in revolt; it is true that if the Duke of Leicester should dare to visit his Irish duchy he would very soon receive four fine bullets in his skull.

But what is the result? In some twenty years' time Leicester's labourers will still be suffering hunger and cold—and the Duke of Leicester's son, himself Duke then, will annually be collecting his four hundred *contos*!

All this cannot change. Human effort may manage at its best to transform a starving proletariat into a well-fed bourgeoisie; but then a worse proletariat emerges from the bowels of society. Jesus was right, there will always be the poor among us. Which proves that this humanity is the greatest error that God ever committed.

Here we are on this world some twelve thousand years wearily circling the sun, and not moving forward an inch along the famous path of progress and perfection, for only some naïve rustic will still consider as progress the idle invention of these puerile toys they call machines, engines, locomotives, etc., and these laborious, diffuse tracts of prose they call *social systems*.

In the first two or three thousand years of existence we reached a considerable height of civilization; but since then we have come hurtling downwards.

The social fabric of Aria, a village in the Himalayas, as it has been preserved up to the present day through ancient tradition, is infinitely more perfect than our domestic and social organism. I am not speaking here of Greeks and Romans: no one today has the genius to compose a chorus like Aeschylus, or a page of Virgil; in terms of architecture and sculpture we are grotesque; no millionaire is capable of dining as Lucullus used to dine; greater ideas were born in one day in Athens or Rome than we could conceive in a century; our armies are derisory compared with the Germanic legions; there is nothing to compare with Roman administration; the *boulevard* is a dirty alley in comparison with the Via Appia; not even an Aspasia have we; nobody will ever speak again like Demosthenes: and serfdom and slavery, this shame of antiquity, was surely no worse than the lot of the modern proletariat.

One could, in fact, say that man is not even superior to

his worthy father the monkey, except in two terrible qualities: moral suffering and social suffering.

God has only one course to take with such useless humanity: drown it with a deluge. But drown it altogether, without repeating the fatal indulgence that led him to spare Noah: if it were not for the senile egoism of this drunken old patriarch, who wanted to go on living so he could go on drinking, we would today enjoy the ineffable happiness of non-existence.

Christmas Literature

ONE OF THE most charming things that Christmas brings us are those lovely children's books which make up what is called Christmas literature.

I am not speaking of those extraordinary gift volumes, published by certain French houses, in decorative covers like the façades of cathedrals, which cost a fortune and carry a text that no one ever reads, and are offered to children but are really a gift to the parents. The poor children get no fun out of these typographical monuments: they are allowed only a glimpse of the engravings, and for this must stand well away from the books, under the supervision of Mama, who is afraid the binding will get spoilt; and the magnificent volume serves to decorate the *jardinière* in the drawing-room, beside the elegant lamp-standard.

In England a real children's literature exists, which has its classics and innovators, a movement and a market, editors and talent—in nothing in fact is it inferior to our own literature for sober adults. Here, no sooner does the little child learn to spell than straightway he has his own special books; they are adorable works, of a dozen or so pages, interspersed with illustrations, printed in enormous letters and edited with rare taste. Generally the subject is a story, in six or seven sentences, and certainly less complicated and dramatic than *The Count of Monte Cristo* or *Nana*; but nevertheless they have their characters and their plots and their moral and their drama.

Such, for example, is the sorry tragedy of the *Three Wise Men of Chester*: they were very old and very wise; and in order to discuss aspects of their wisdom, they squeezed themselves into a barrel, but a shepherd that came running after a sheep tumbled against the barrel, and the three wise men of Chester were left standing on their heads!

There are thousands like this: *The Diverting History of John Gilpin* is a masterpiece.

Then, when the infant reaches eight or nine, another type of literature is offered him. The wise men, the barrel, the tumbles, no longer capture their interest; now they want books on travel and hunting and shipwrecks, about courageous heroes, a salutary chronicle of triumph, of human effort against nature's resistance.

All this is told in a simple language, pure and clear— and proving the point that in life success always belongs to those with energy, discipline, *sang-froid* and goodness. Rarely is the child taken to wonderland: there is little in this literature of phantoms or miracles or caverns containing gold-scaled dragons: this is kept for the grown-ups. And when fairies or angels are spoken of it is in such a way that the child will naturally laugh at this picturesque suggestion of the supernatural, and consider it in the same light as he considers his own little toy lambs.

What the books sometimes do is animate the inanimate companions of infancy with a fictitious life: dolls and puppets and lead soldiers. There will be the story, for example, of the adventures of an honest but unhappy doll: or the sufferings that a box of lead soldiers went through during a campaign in a far-off war. This literature is profound. The privations of real soldiers would not perhaps interest a child—but all his heart goes out when he reads of the suffering and misery endured by his little friends, his lead warriors, whose twisted bayonets his fingers are straightening all day long: and in this way a horror of war can be implanted in the child's mind.

The moral lessons given in this way are innumerable, and all the more successful when they originate in the life and action of the beings that he knows best—his toys.

After this there are further books for readers of twelve to fifteen years: explanations of the sciences; dramatic descriptions of the Universe; enthralling studies of the world of plants and sea and birds; voyages and discoveries; history; and finally, in works of fiction, social life is presented carefully lest an unduly crude picture of reality nourish feelings of misanthropy in the tender spirit, or false idealization produce morbid sentimentality.

It is mainly at Christmas that this literature flourishes. The book-shop windows are a paradise then. There is nothing more picturesque, more original, more decorative, than English book-bindings; and the illustrations, the pale tones and water-colours, are almost always real works of art, charm and humour.

I do not know if this type of literature exists in Brazil. In Portugal I have never even heard it mentioned. One or two of those luxury editions from Paris may appear, on which I have already commented and which are no more than drawing-room adornments. France also has a children's literature as rich and useful as the English; but Portugal is not interested in this sort of publication: books to complete the furnishing, yes, but to educate the spirit, oh dear no!

Belgium, Holland, Germany, abound in these books for children; in Denmark and Sweden they are the pride of their literature and occupy a profitable place on the market.

Nothing of this in Portugal.

Sometimes I wonder what the poor children do read in Portugal. I believe they give them Filinto Elísio, Garção, or some other tasteless dullard when the poor things show an inclination to read.

This is even more atrocious when the Portuguese child is extremely lively, intelligent and imaginative. In general, we Portuguese only begin to be idiotic when we reach the age of reason. While we are young we all have a spark of genius: and I am certain that if a children's literature existed as it does in Sweden or Holland, to mention only countries as small as our own, there would be a considerable rise in our standard of intelligence.

Instead of this, scarcely does the light of understanding begin to glow in our children than we bury it under heavy layers of Latin! After Latin we add rhetoric! After rhetoric we pile on logic (logic, of all things!) And so we go on building up and up to the Heavens this monument of nonsense!

I am sure that a more youthful literature would swiftly penetrate our domestic habits and would make profitable sales. Many women, intelligent and poor, could be employed in creating these simple stories: we do not need a

Zola or a Thackeray to invent the tale of the three wise men of Chester. We have many artists who wield a light, inventive brush to complement these adventures with simple illustrations done in bright colours . . . And think of the thousands of children who would find pleasure in these pretty books—which, if they are to be popular and cheap enough to tear without regret, should cost almost nothing!

I am well aware that this idea of composing books purely for children would make all Lisbon laugh. But I am not offering the idea to Lisbon. Lisbon would not bother with details such as these.

Lisbon wants something superior; it wants the beautiful lyrical stanza, the ornate drama where the hero dies heart-broken in the moonlight, the sentimental *étude* on the piano, the courtship on the stairs, the plaintive dirge, the violent midnight stabbing, the Andalusian of the long tresses, talk of Golgotha—everything in fact which stems from the noblest inventions of Portuguese romanticism. To attempt to educate their children intelligently is surely beneath their dignity.

However, if these lines encourage a writer, an artist and an editor somewhere in Brazil or in a Portuguese colony, to prepare some good, light-hearted, humorous books for little children—then I shall have done the Empire a colossal service for which I cannot see how they can sufficiently reward me.

A fine estate, with a guaranteed income, in a wealthy province, with a furnished house and horses in the stables, would not perhaps be too much. If the Imperial Government's gratitude should wish to add a few million in gold as pin-money, I should not refuse. Or if they did not wish to give me anything, then I should be content that one little child should laugh and have a few moments' pleasure. Considering the matter carefully, I think the latter would be the reward I preferred.

Israelism

THE TWO GREAT 'sensations' of the month are un-doubtedly the publication of Lord Beaconsfield's new novel *Endymion*, and the agitation in Germany against the Jews. From the literary and social viewpoint, then, this month belongs to the Israelites. This extraordinary anti-Jewish movement, this incredible resurrection of the pious wrath of the sixteenth century, is followed with a great deal of interest here in England, for Jews abound here as well as in Germany, exerting influence on public opinion through the newspapers they own, (the *Daily Telegraph* among others, one of the most important in the kingdom), controlling trade through their banking houses and at times even governing the State through the great man of their race, their major prophet, Lord Beaconsfield himself. Here we are certainly far from seeing national hatred break out, and social persecution of the Jews; but there are sufficient signs that the steady development of this Israelite state, within the Christian state, is beginning to irritate the Englishman. I cannot see, for example, that what is happening in Germany, in spite of the dreadful stench of an auto-da-fé that it gives off, is causing very much indignation in the liberal London press: and a paper of such authority as the *Spectator* has already been compelled to modify, after

45

protests from the Israelite colony, articles in which it had described the Jews as a self-centred, isolated body, similar to Catholic communities, working only for their own interest, shutting themselves up in the strength of their tradition, and holding sympathies and tendencies hostile to the State which tolerates them. This is all very disagreeable.

But what shall we say about the movement in Germany? That in 1880, in wise, tolerant Germany, heir to Hegel and Kant and Schopenhauer, with Professors Strauss and Hartmann alive and active, a campaign should once more be started against the Jew, the killer of Christ, as if the Emperor Maximilian were still, from his camp at Padua, decreeing the destruction of the Rabbinic Law, and the furious 'Pepper-Corn', the Dominican General, were still preaching in Cologne—here is a fact to make one stand open-mouthed in disbelief a whole long summer's day . . . Because what it really is that we are witnessing, under its civilized, constitutional cover of petitions, magazine articles, pamphlets and speeches, is a persecution of Jews, one of the old variety, the Manueline sort, when they used to fling Rabbinic books and the Rabbi himself onto the same bonfire, thus exterminating, economically, with the same bundle of wood, doctrine and doctor.

And it is a strange and edifying spectacle to see the venerable Professor Virchow getting up in the German parliament to defend the Jews, the wisdom of the Hebrew books, the synagogues, refuge of ideas during barbaric times—exactly as the worthy lawyer Roenchlin defended them during the persecutions which closed the fifteenth century!

But still more extraordinary is the German government's attitude: summoned to give the official opinion, the State opinion, on this sudden and obsolete rancour of Germany against the Jew, the government has merely declared, with dry and sparing comment, 'that it has no intention for the moment of altering legislation concerning Israelites'! One would, indeed, scarcely expect the ministers of the Empire, philosophers and professors, to decree, like D. Manuel, the expulsion of the Jews, or restrict their civil liberty so as to isolate them in remote streets, shut in by iron chains like in the Ghetto. But a declaration such as this is no less threatening. The State merely lets it be known that any persecution will not be encouraged on its own initiative: it does not utter a single word, however, to condemn this strange anti-Semitic movement, which in many aspects is now organized by its own officials.

It leaves the Jewish colony unprotected to face the anger of the large German population—and washes its ministerial hands, as Pontius Pilate did.

It does not even state that it will see that the laws protecting the Jews, citizens of the Empire, are enforced; it merely has the vague intention, as vague as a morning cloud, of not altering them *for the moment*!

What is the result in a nation where the conservative society forms a sort of large battalion and thinks whatever the 'order of the day' tells them, and marches in disciplined fashion to their Colonel's command? Every good German, every patriot, is going to conclude immediately from such ambiguous language of the government that if the Court, the General Staff, the Field-

47

marshals, Mr Bismarck and all this respected and obeyed body do not actually view hatred of Jewry with enthusiasm, neither do they disapprove of it in their Christian hearts ... And the new movement will surely receive unexpected encouragement from this.

What am I saying? It has already received it. No sooner had the government's reply been made known than a group of youths in Leipzig, who might have been Dominican friars, but who were really philosophy students, went round the beer halls turning out the Jews, denying them the dearest and most sacred individual right of any German: his right to beer!

But why this hatred of the Jew? Germany surely does not wish to start avenging the precious blood of Jesus again. These painful things happened such a long time ago! Christian humanity is old now, and therefore indulgent: eighteen centuries is long enough to forget the deepest affront. And unfortunately there is no one today who will furiously draw his sword like Clovis and shout, with tears streaming down his cheeks: 'Infamous rogues! Would that I had been there with my Franks!'

Apart from which, this movement is organized by the bourgeoisie, and the conservative classes of Germany are too juridically-minded not to approve, in their innermost thoughts, Jesus's punishment. When you have an ancient and prosperous society, with its official religion, its official code of morals, its official literature, its clergy, its system of private property, its aristocracy and its trade— what can you do with a fellow inspired by God, a revolutionary, who suddenly appears followed by an unruly mob, and preaches the destruction of these sacred institutions, and upon its ruins the foundation of a new social order—what is known in legal language as inciting the hatred of the people against the government? Evidently he must be punished.

This is required by law and order, by the State, by public safety and conservative interests. It is precisely what Germany, with due reason, does to its socialists Karl Marx and Bebel. Now these wicked men certainly have no desire to start a revolution in contemporary Germany any more radical than the one Jesus undertook in the semitic world. It is true that the Nazarene was a God—for us, anyway, privileged humanity who have learnt to love and understand him. But in Jerusalem, for the doctor of the Temple, for the scribe, for the merchant in David's quarter, for the owner of the cornfields that stretched as far as Bethlehem, for the stern Centurion charged with maintaining order—Jesus was merely a rebel.

And if Bismarck were wearing the toga, in the praetorium, seated in the curule chair of Caiaphas, he would have signed the fatal sentence as serenely as the afore-mentioned Caiaphas, certain that at that moment he was saving his country from anarchy. The conservatives of Jerusalem were logical and legal, as they are in Berlin today or in St Petersburg or Vienna: in the ancient world, as today, there were the same sacred interests to guard. What the deuce! It is indispensable that the basic structures of society should be maintained, and formerly, as today, the preservation of order is the justification of punishment.

It is possible that this pleasure we conservatives derive

from crushing our socialist Messiahs, imprisoning our Proudhons, sending Bacunins to Siberia and crushing our Felix Pyats with fines—will cost our grandchildren dear. As time goes on every great social reformer is gradually transformed into a God: Zoroaster, Confucius, Mohamet, and Jesus are all recent examples! Superior forms of thought have a fatal tendency of later becoming revealed law: and all philosophy ends, in its last stages, by becoming religion. Auguste Comte already has altars to him in London; already he is prayed to. And as today we demand chapels to the Fathers of the Church, to those who were the holy authors, the noble creators of Catholicism, perhaps one day, when socialism is the State religion, there will be niches in the temples, with a little lamp in front, and inside, images of the Fathers of the Revolution: Proudhon complete with glasses, Bacunin looking like a bear under his Russian pelts, Karl Marx leaning on his staff—symbolic of the shepherd of souls.

As civilization is travelling towards the West, this will all happen somewhere about the twenty-eighth century in New Zealand or Australia, when we, in our turn, will be the ancient races of the East, our languages dead ones, and Paris and London mountains of truncated columns like Palmira and Babylon are today, which the New Zealander and Australian will come to visit in his balloon, on a return ticket . . . Logically then, as today in Germany the heirs of those that killed Jesus are detested, so there will be only repulsion and hatred for the descendants of us who are at present imprisoning Bacunin, or fining Pyat. And as all religion has a period of frenzy and destruction, these our poor descendants will be persecuted and will become the race which is cursed and will die of the punishments their enemies will inflict . . . *C'est raide*!

*

But to get back to Germany.

Although the Peter the Hermit of this new constitutional crusade is a priest, the Rev. Streker, chaplain and court preacher, it is evident that he does not draw his strength from religious passion. Jesus's five wounds have nothing to do with these petitions that are being signed all over the place, begging the government to stop the Jews from acquiring property, and being admitted to public offices and other Gothic extravagances! The motive of this anti-Semitic fury is simply the growing prosperity of the Jewish colony, a relatively small colony, composed of some four hundred thousand Jews, but who, by their activity, their pertinacity, their discipline, are becoming triumphant rivals of the German middle-class.

High finance and small business are both in their hands: it is the Jew who lends to the State and to princes, and it is to him that the small land-owner mortgages his land. In the liberal professions he absorbs everything: he is the lawyer with more briefs and the doctor with more patients; if there are two shopkeepers in the same street, one a German and one a Jew, it will be Germany's son who will be bankrupt by the end of the year, and the son of Israel who will have a carriage! This has become even more striking since the war: and the good German cannot tolerate this spectacle of the Jew growing fatter and richer while he, crowned with laurels, has to emigrate to America for his bread.

But if the Jew's wealth irritates him, the show the Jew makes of his riches absolutely maddens him. And I must say that on this point the German has a certain amount of reason. The old picture of the Israelite as a tall, slightly bowed, lean fellow, creeping along close to the wall, with a secret, suspicious glance lurking beneath his eyelids— that all belongs to the past. The Jew today is a fat man. He holds his head high, has a prominent paunch and fills the street. One has to see them in London, in Berlin, or in Vienna: in the most trivial things, entering a café, or taking their seat at the theatre, they have an arrogant and ostentatious attitude which is scandalous. Their showy pomp like so many *parvenu* Solomons offends our contemporary sense of decency, which is very sober. They always talk loud as if treading a conquered land, and in a London or Berlin restaurant there is nothing more intolerable than Semitic chatter. They cover themselves with jewels, all the trappings of their carriages are of gold, and they love vulgar and showy luxury. All this is irritating.

But worse still, in Germany, is their skilful manner of strengthening their prosperity and guaranteeing their influence—so skilful a plan that it has a taste of conspiracy about it: in Germany, the Jew has slowly and stealthily gained possession of two great social forces— the Exchange and the Press. Almost all the big banking houses in Germany, almost all the big newspapers are in the Semite's possession. He thus becomes inexpugnable. So not only do they expel the German from the liberal professions, humiliate him by their scintillating opulence, hold him dependent on their capital; but, supreme insult, the voice of their newspapers tells him what he must do, what he must think, how he should be governed and with whom he must fight!

All this would still be bearable if the Jew merged with the indigenous race. But no. The Jewish world keeps itself isolated, compact, inaccessible and impenetrable. The formidable walls of Solomon's temple which were once demolished, continue to create an obstacle of fortresses around it. Within Berlin there is a real impregnable Jerusalem: there they take refuge with their God, their Book, their customs, their Sabbath, their language, their pride, their very astringency, enjoying their gold and despising the Christians. They invade German society, want to shine there and dominate it, but they do not allow the German to put one little step inside Jewish society. So they marry within their race; within it they help each other regally, millions passing from one to another—but they would not favour a starving German with a pfennig; and they take a pride, an insolent pride, in being different from the rest of the nation in everything, from their way of thinking to their way of dress. Naturally, so accentuated an exclusiveness is interpreted as hostility—and repaid with hatred.

All this, however, is the struggle for existence. The Jew is the stronger, the Jew is triumphant. What the German should do is exercise his muscle, sharpen his wits, make an effort, push forward until he, in his turn, is the stronger. He does not do this: instead of this, he turns miserably, cowardly, to the Government and begs, on great sheets of paper, that the Jew be deprived of his rights, because the Jew is rich and the Jew is strong.

＊

The government rubs its hands, and beams. The English newspapers do not understand Mr Bismarck's attitude, his tacitly approving the anti-Jewish movement. It is simple to understand; it is a streak of genius of the Chancellor's. Or at least a proof that he reads his History of Germany profitably.

In the Middle Ages, every time that an excess of public misfortunes, plague or hunger, drove the population to despair; every time that enslaved man, crushed and exploited, showed signs of revolt, the Church and the Prince hastened to tell it: 'We see only too well that you are suffering! But it is your own fault! The fact is the Jews killed Our Lord and you have not yet punished them sufficiently.' Then the population would fling itself upon the Jews: they beheaded them, they burnt them, they quartered them, they had an orgy of punishments until, sated, the mob withdrew into the gloom of their wretchedness to wait for the Lord's reward.

This never failed. Whenever the Church or the feudal lords felt themselves threatened by a mob which was straining desperately at its painful yoke—they diverted the blow from themselves and redirected it towards the Jew.

When the bestial mob showed a thirst for blood—it helped itself from the vulgar Israelite blood.

This is precisely what Mr Bismarck is doing to a more

civilized extent. Germany is suffering and muttering: the prolonged trade crisis, the bad harvests, the excessive taxes, the lengthy military service, industrial deterioration—all this irritates the middle class. The people, who suffer more, at least have a hope in socialism; but the conservatives begin to see that their misfortunes stem from their idols.

The best thing to calm and occupy it, and thus help the Chancellor, would be a war, but a war cannot always be invented, and it is becoming no light undertaking to meet France on the battle-field—a France ably-prepared, stronger than ever, with her two million excellent soldiers, her fabulous wealth, an inconceivable wealth which, as the *Saturday Review* said a few days ago, is a disquieting phenomenon and one not easy to explain.

Therefore, with little chance of a war, Prince Bismarck distracts the starving Germans' attention—by pointing to the prosperous Jew. Naturally he does not allude to the death of Our Lord Jesus Christ. But he speaks of the millions of Jews and the power of the Synagogue. And this explains the government's strange and disastrous declaration.

*

Concerning the other 'sensation'—Lord Beaconsfield's novel, *Endymion*—I have no room left for laughter in this letter. It includes among its characters, under transparent names, Beaconsfield himself, Napoleon III, Prince Bismarck, Cardinal Manning, the Rothschilds, the Empress Eugénie, duchesses, lords and marshals . . .

55

Quite a bouquet altogether, for which its editor, Longman, paid *fifty-four contos.*

My friends, young men of letters, look carefully upon this golden example! Be prudent, young man; never, when entering upon a literary career, publish poem or story without first taking the precaution of being for some years Prime Minister of England!

Afghanistan and Ireland

IN THEIR TROUBLED Indian Empire the English are attempting to discover whether there is any truth in the eighteenth-century witticism that 'History is like an old woman who keeps on repeating herself.'

Fate, or Providence, or whatever Being it is up there that directed the events of the Afghanistan campaign in 1847, is simply making a slavish copy now, thus apparently showing an exhausted imagination.

In 1847 the English, 'for a reason of State, a need for scientific frontiers, the security of the Empire, a barrier to the Russian dominion of Asia . . .' and other vague things that the politicians concerned with India solemnly mutter as they twist their moustaches—invaded Afghanistan, and proceeded to annihilate ancient tribes, destroy towns, lay waste cornfields and vineyards; finally they took possession of the holy city of Kabul: they turned out a terrified old Emir from the Seraglio and installed another of a more submissive race, whom they had brought with them ready in their baggage, along with some slave-girls and carpets; and as soon as the newspaper correspondents cabled the victory, the army camped beside the streams and in the gardens of Kabul, undid their belts and smoked the pipe of peace . . . And that is exactly what is happening in 1880.

At the moment, precisely as in 1847, energetic leaders, native Messiahs, are travelling through this territory and with fine words like Homeland and Religion, are inciting their brethren to a holy war: the tribes are assembling, feudal families hasten to offer their mounted troops, rival princes join forces in their hereditary hatred for the foreigner, and in a short time all will be a-glimmer with the lights of encampments on the hill-tops overlooking the narrow paths which form the route to India . . . And when the bulk of the English army appears on the approaches to Kabul, with a mass of artillery, and makes its hurried way through narrow passes in the mountains or along the dry river beds, with its long caravans of camels, the savage horde falls upon them and annihilates them.

So it was in 1847 and so it is again in 1880. The disbanded remains of the army then seek refuge in one of the frontier cities, which might be Ghazni or Kandahar: the Afghans rush in pursuit, and set siege to them, a slow siege, an Oriental, leisurely siege: the besieged general, who in these Asiatic wars can always communicate with the outside world, cables to the Viceroy of India, indignantly demanding *reinforcements, sugar and tea*! (This is literally true: it was General Roberts who made this gluttonous British appeal a few days ago; the Englishman without his tea fights only half-heartedly.) Then the Indian government spends millions of pounds like water, and hastily sends off enormous parcels of restorative tea and white mountains of sugar and ten or fifteen thousand men. Enormous black war-transports leave England, like great steam-powered Noah's arks, carrying camping equipment, numerous horses, parks of artillery, a complete, awesome invading force. So it was in 1847, and so it is in 1880.

This host disembarks in Hindustan, joins up with other columns of Indian troops, and is led day and night to the frontier in express trains at a speed of 40 miles an hour; then an exhausting march begins with fifty thousand pack-camels, telegraphists, hydraulic machines, and an eloquent company of newspaper men. One morning Kandahar or Ghazni is sighted; and in a flash the poor Afghan army is wiped out, dispersed in the dust of the plain, with its melodramatic scimitars and its venerable culverins of the same model that fired in former days at Diu. Ghazni is liberated! Kandahar is liberated! Hurrah! Immediately a patriotic song is made of this, and the exploit is popularized all over England by an engraving where the liberating general and the besieged general can be seen passionately shaking hands in the foreground, amid rearing horses and Grenadiers as handsome as Apollo who are nobly breathing their last! So it was in 1847; so it must be in 1880.

In the meantime, on hill-tops and narrow paths, thousands of men who either defended their homeland or died for the sake of the *scientific frontier*, lie there, food for the crows—which is not, in Afghanistan, a respectable rhetorical image: there it is the crows which clean up the streets in the cities, eating the filth, and on the battlefield purify the air by devouring the remains of the defeated.

And what is eventually left after so much blood and agony and mourning? A patriotic song, an idiotic

59

engraving in a few dining rooms, later on a line of prose in a page of some chronicle . . .

A consoling philosophy of wars!

In the meantime England enjoys the prestige of 'the great victory of Afghanistan' for a short while—certain of having to begin it once more in ten or fifteen years, because they can neither conquer and annex a vast kingdom, as large as France, nor allow the existence of a few million hostile fanatics at their side. Their policy, therefore, is to weaken them periodically with a devastating invasion: such violence is required of a great Empire. Far better to possess only a little garden with a cow for milk and a couple of lettuces for summer snacks . . .

*

Another melancholy story is that of Ireland. Everyone is familiar with the age-old laments of Ireland, of Green Erin, land of bards and saints, where a conquered people, the noble remains of a Celtic race, crushed by an agrarian feudalism and living in holes as the Gothic serfs did, desperately snatch from heather and rocks and marshland scraps of soil where in tears and sweat they cultivate the potato. Everyone knows this legend—and unfortunately this Ireland of story and poem is partly true: apart from the few areas where the agriculture is as rich as in any of the most fertile counties of England, and apart from Belfast and Cork which are industrialized—Ireland remains the land of poverty well-represented in the romantic engraving which shows her lying in rags at the edge of a pool, with her little son dying at her breast for lack of milk and her dog at her side, as skinny as she, barking in vain for help.

Ireland's ills, long standing and highly complex, stem principally from the semi-feudal system of property.

The Irish people are numerous and inordinately prolific (neither emigration nor death nor epidemics relieve this overcrowded little island) and they live in a poor land of meagre yield with only a third of it cultivated: the proprietors, Scottish or English lords, always absent from their lands and never allowing a shilling to be spent to improve them, are in Paris or in London, eating peaches in January, and playing whist in their clubs staking a pound a time: their agents and bailiffs—voracious creatures utterly foreign to the soil and the race, forced to send money incessantly to their lordships and interested only in holding on to their positions—fall upon the tenant, put up his rent, force him to disastrous sales, get him entangled in usury, exact feudal tributes, and squeeze him mercilessly like a half-dry lemon, until with a groan he gives up his last penny. If the poor wretch this year, by exhausting his strip of soil and keeping himself alive on dried grass and economizing on the fire when there is six feet of snow, manages to scrape together the sum which His Lordship requires to offer an emerald to fair Fanny or pale Clementine, next year he is stuck in debt with no means to buy seed and with an exhausted soil at his feet.

Then the agent, with the law behind him, comes running, distrains his goods and chattels, sells his pallet, evicts him from his humble home, and flings his wife and children and invalid grandparents out on to the street . . .

And that means one more group of poor devils to swell the lamentable number of beggars who people the Bards' Green Isle. There are thousands of them, millions! This population, with its stomach empty and its feet bare on the frosty road, then turns to England, England the Motherland, which has the Law, and the strength and the responsibility: England, her Christian compassion touched, turns to her economists and her politicians: these individuals fold their enormous hands and wrench from the depths of their Pharisaic wisdom this reply, a gloomy middle-aged reply to the demands of human suffering:

'Have patience! Heaven has the answer . . .'

England, taking full advantage of the Catholic clergy of Ireland, and of the religious feeling of the masses, to keep them resignedly accepting their misery, fobbing them off with golden promises of blessedness—what an edifying spectacle!

Let us, however, be fair: England does send flour and a few shillings to the millions of starving Irish: and *Punch* honours them by making a few jokes about them.

And what is the result of all this? The Irishman, seeing his family hungry and the English occupied with Dr Tanner, and *Punch* highly amused and Heaven far away, bundles up his rags, goes to the nearest town and presents himself to the *Fenians* Committee, or the local section of *Mollie Maguire*, and says simply, 'Here I am!'

These two secret associations are terrible and complement each other. The *Fenians*, who were at one time disorganized but now have the prosperity of a public institution, are a political group with the clear purpose of

62

gaining Ireland's independence: its aim is insurrection, battles in broad daylight and a heroic effort of the whole race to shake off the foreigner.

England clearly has nothing to fear from this association: a squadron in St George's Channel, a disembarkation of ten thousand men, and the *Fenians* would be, as the song goes, like the grass of the fields after the cutter passes, a stretch of lifeless things! But this is not the case with *Mollie Maguire*, which is pure conspiracy: its statutes, its aims, its organization, its leaders, everything is wrapped in a mystery which spells terror in Ireland: all that is clear are her crimes. Is there a hard-hearted landowner who has raised the rent? One night, either he or his agent will be found by the roadside with a couple of bullets through his head. Who was it? It was *Mollie Maguire*: it was no one, it was misery, it was Ireland. Is there a landlord, or an agent of his, who has made a seizure of someone's goods? At midnight his house begins to burn and a few moments later it is a smoking ruin. Who was it? *Mollie Maguire*. Was there some speculating citizen who bought the humble home of a distrained holder of a patch of land? The following day there he is at the bottom of a lake with a large stone tied round his neck. Who was it, poor fellow? Why, *Mollie Maguire*. Every day these last few months, it has been like this, two or three cases of this type of crime—which in England are termed agrarian outrages. The courts, the police, no longer waste their time in inquests and enquiries: what for? *Mollie Maguire* is intangible, *Mollie Maguire* is impersonal.

And if there were a magistrate so unloving of life that

he should wish to discover who supplied the bullet or the stone or the fire—he would surely have all he could desire a few short hours later: a dagger in his breast. These are the very actions of a militant nihilism: and this sect is not without the vague mystic exaltation which can be a feature of nihilism. If Mollie (Mollie is the diminutive of Mary) is not a divinity, she is at least a fetishistic degeneration of the divinity: she is the gloomy patron saint of the people's revenge, where those unfortunate ones abandoned by God, by the official God, by the God of the Mass, find help and friendship and strength—a sort of Sabbath witch, reliant on her midnight servants and magicians.

To these two associations must be added a third, a legal one this time, which speaks in public and has newspapers and a name-plate, and lives under the protection of the Constitution, is respected by the police and is called the Land League. Its aim is to promote, by dint of meetings, a great surge of opinion, a vast agitation, which would force the English Parliament to reform the Agrarian System. But is it really so legal an association? Are its aims as honestly moderate, as strictly constitutional as it says? Everyone doubts this. In Ireland, whenever two men get together they conspire; when they find their number is four, they begin stoning the police. What will they do then, when they find they are two hundred thousand? Apart from this, the demands of this association are singularly vague: nothing practical, nothing achievable, only the old sentimental cries of a humanitarian aspiration. And, at the same time, the men who direct them are positive and experienced souls. There is a frightening

64

contradiction here. One feels that the leaders of this movement, well aware that they can expect nothing from England, are simply, under the appearances of legality, organizing insurrection. To formulate a practical programme for Parliament to vote on would be, in their opinion, idle and puerile: the verbose declarations, the talk about *legality, order, parliamentarianism,* are sufficient to deceive the police . . . And there is no doubt that, at a certain moment, *Fenians, Mollie Maguire* and the *Land League* will unite to form a single movement—that of desperate revolt.

This was the state of Ireland some two months ago, when the unexpected Compensation for Disturbance Bill appeared. This was introduced by the Minister Gladstone (partly by a liberal sense of justice, partly to thank the Irish for their strong support in the last elections) and would by no means have brought Ireland's problems to an end; but by restraining the landlords' abuses, by modifying the barbaric legislation of the distraints, it would have relieved the Irish worker from the feudal iron heel which was crushing him. The Bill passed the House of Commons amid applause; I need hardly add that the Lords, that august and Gothic assembly of semi-feudal lords, rejected it with horror, like some execrable work of Satanic liberalism!

And what is the result? The agitators of Ireland, their prophets and leaders, enthusiastically welcomed this rejection by the House of Lords—and they have used it as skilfully as Anthony used Caesar's bloody tunic. They have gone round the fields and villages showing it to the indignant people, crying aloud: 'Here is what your Lords, your masters, your exploiters have done! You must reject, in the name of Ireland, the first fair proposal they offer you! They want to keep you in servitude, in hunger, in the disgraceful state of ages past, in the state of a dispossessed race. To arms!'

And since then, Ireland has been preparing herself for insurrection: in spite of the cruisers that watch the coast, arms are landed every day; money and volunteers are provided in plenteous supply by America; groups of two or three hundred men can be seen marching through the countryside, rifles at their shoulders, on exercises like regiments on the eve of battle. Although it is now harvest-time the population is not in the fields but at meetings, at clubs, and the tribunes and agitators exhaust themselves mercilessly. These men certainly do not lack courage or the sort of pathetic eloquence that stirs the listening crowds. One of them exclaimed a few days ago:

'They are always telling us: "be fair, pay His Lordship, pay your landlord!" And they quote the divine word which says: "Render to Caesar the things that are Caesar's." There was only one man, Brutus, who gave Caesar his due: and that was a dagger through his heart!'

This brutality has a grandeur about it. Now imagine this ringing out to an oppressed crowd, with the theatrical gestures typical of this violent race, at night, on one of those sinister stretches of wasteland in Ireland, which are all heather and rocks, in the light of torches, with their intermittent flashes of light and gloom, like the very soul of Ireland—and see the effect!

In England even the optimists consider insurrection almost inevitable by the time the cold begins in autumn.

And honest John Bull is getting ready: already the Minister of Home Affairs is in Dublin and declaration of martial law is imminent ... On this point radicals and conservatives are unanimous: if Ireland rebels, Ireland must be crushed! Only John Bull declares that his heart will weep while his hand administers punishment ... An excellent father!

The *Standard*, the worthy *Standard*, used a delightful phrase a few days ago. 'If, as is feared, Ireland should forget what she owes herself and England,' exclaimed the solemn *Standard*, 'it is painful to think that next winter, to maintain the integrity of the Empire, the sacredness of law and the inviolability of property, we shall have to go, our heart heavy with sorrow but our sword firm in our hands, and carry out in Ireland, our sister isle, that well-beloved isle, a necessary extermination.'

Extermination is a harsh word: and I should like to believe that it was put there to finish off the sentence harmoniously with the proper grave organ-like note. But the sentiment is curious and rare: it would be a marvellous spectacle to see, next winter, John Bull marching through Ireland, full of ferocity and bathed in tenderness, with tears streaming from his eyes and blood streaming from his bayonet ... The fatal requirements of a great empire again! I return to my preference: a little garden, a cow, a couple of lettuces ... And a pipe—the pipe of peace!

Ireland and the
Land League

I MUST SPEAK of Ireland, of the Land League, of Parnell . . .

For the last six months, this man, this association and this isle of unrest have been the chief concern, the most acute worry of England and of all thinking Englishmen, from statesmen to cartoonists. And soon European opinion, world opinion, will grow excited about the Irish Problem, as it formerly did about the Polish Problem.

The Polish Problem! Oh, those ardent days of the past! It was one of my first enthusiasms. At that time, to be Polish was synonymous with being a hero: and the more usual form of passion in a twenty-year-old consisted not in the desire to climb up to Juliet's balcony, but to set out and take up arms for Poland. In Coimbra, whenever four or more friends got together, we immediately made this sort of plan, shouting 'Long live Poland!' The papers were full of poems dedicated to Poland and insults to the Bear of the North! Gowns and dictionaries were pawned so that enthusiastic subscriptions might be raised to help Poland. In aid of Poland I acted in many a melodrama: in one, a betrayed virgin dressed in white, with long locks floating loose and sobs in my throat; in another, a traitor uttering loud cynical laughs as I plunged my sword into the Count's breast!

But we were no more absurd than the people of Paris who, in 1848, marched in procession to their provisional government demanding the liberation of Poland. 'But it would mean a war with Russia, a major European conflict!' argued the more prudent. And the enthusiasts replied, 'Don't worry; France is the Messiah, she is the saviour of the oppressed: France is the Christ among nations; if it were necessary she would die for them.'

But since 1848 much water has passed under the bridges, as they say in Paris; and much blood too.

At these times of opportunism and naturalism, poor Ireland will never inspire the pious fervour that Poland did in former days.

Also Poland and Ireland are two quite different cases. It is undeniable that, seen from a distance, through the misty haze of sentiment, they offer similarities. Ireland might perhaps be considered a constitutional Poland: as in Poland, there is an oppressed race here, whose soil was divided between the great vassals, the historic families of the conquering nation; and it has long been under the rule of the great land-owners. Only in Ireland the abuses, the high-handedness which this situation produces are covered, through the parliamentary regime, by a beautiful varnish of legality: and Ireland suffers the miseries of a conquered and exploited country—but within constitutional laws.

The Irishman is like the Pole in certain aspects: they are both impulsive and imprudent, courageous, generous and poetic. Like the Poles, the Catholic Irish detest the conqueror, above all else because he is a heretic by nationality, thus adding religious conflict to political hatred. As in Poland there is in Ireland the patriotic legend of independence, of suppressed revolts, of heroic agitators, a legend which appeals to the popular imagination as much as religion itself, inspiring the same sort of fanaticism, so that the Irishman is as devoted to his saints as to his patriots; as the Pole despises the Russian, so the Irishman considers the Anglo-Saxon as a barbarian, a stupid fellow, and he bears him all the disdainful aversion that a race of improvisors can have for a race of critics and analysts. In the social order, as in the domestic, there are other curious affinities between Poles and Irish. Ireland's latest tactic, in fact, is imitated from Poland: Ireland is going to appeal to Europe and it is Victor Hugo who will speak in her name, in a manifesto bearing the title 'The Oppressed Oppressor.'

But England is not really at all like Russia: not even through the foggy sensitivity and passion which attaches to Ireland's cause, can the most enlightened of liberal regimes be compared with the most ignorant of despotic ones. And yet England, rather than disturb the tyrannic interests of a thousand or so rich landlords, leaves four million men in misery. It has all Irish territory occupied by soldiers. As soon as a patriot begins to have some influence in Ireland they arrest that patriot. When the eloquence of the Irish deputies becomes embarrassing they silence it, breaking without any scruples a centuries-old parliamentary tradition. They are going to govern Ireland by martial law, as a Czar might do. And in order to suspend the plans of the Land League they violate the secrets of letters.

*

This question of Ireland is as complex and confusing as chaos itself before Jehovah's great intervention. First, there are in Ireland three distinct nations with contradictory interests: the Catholic Irish, the Protestant Irish or Orangemen, and the English and Scottish landowners. The question of property is undoubtedly the most essential: but others do exist—the religious question, the political question, the juridical question, the municipal question, etc., etc. And on each of these questions it is difficult to find two Irishmen who agree. Every village has thus become a battle-ground: and as they are eloquent and sarcastic, volubility and love of the epigram intensify and embitter their quarrels.

Even within the Catholic Church, which should preserve the tradition of Unity, discord is rife: the parochial clergy is at war with the episcopal dignitaries: and it is rare that the clergy of one county does not disagree both in sentiments and sermons with the clergy of the neighbouring county. Among its revolutionary patriots no better harmony exists: the Land League will not accept the Fenians and the Fenians detest the parliamentary tendencies of the Home-rulers: and even within the party of Home-rulers, there are democrats and conservatives. An immense conflict spreads across the whole of poor Ireland.

The Irish, however, say that were they given autonomy, all these questions would resolve themselves a few hours after the Irish Republic was declared, and the country would be like a raging sea which grows calm.

But it is this lack of unity which has up to now been offered as evidence of the dangers that autonomy would hold.

The English sincerely believe that the moment Ireland escaped from the protection of English good sense and wisdom, the instant that this impressionable, excited, fanatic and uncultured race were left to its own devices, a civil war would begin, a religious war, different agrarian wars, which would very soon transform Green Erin into a heap of ruins in a pool of blood.

If the Irish are not in agreement about Ireland's misfortunes, the English are even less sure about remedies for Ireland. And the confusion comes mainly from the abundance of discussion. There is no town or even village in England which has not got its own newspaper, the size of our *Gazeta de Notícias*, with eight pages of small print. And this vast expanse of paper, since the beginning of the agitation of the Land League, has been filled from top to bottom with articles and studies on Ireland. Multiply this by the three or four thousand gazettes which poor England nourishes under her tender skin: add to this the articles of weekly papers, of fortnightly papers, of the reviews and magazines, the pamphlets, the brochures, the essays which are as innumerable as the stars in Heaven, the books and treatises of every sort imaginable, speeches in Parliament, talks at meetings, lectures, sermons, public debates—all the enormous literature, in fact, which in these last months has taken Ireland as its theme.

And tell me whether it is not natural, with all this wealth of information, of theories, of projects, of systems, of opinions and imaginings—that England's brain is reeling on this question of Ireland. Mine is. But I have illustrious companions in this mental chaos: the great Carlyle used to say that the sincerity and high-mindedness of some Irish patriots was the only clear and lucid thing which he could distinguish in the tumultuous gloom of the Irish tangle.

There is another thing we cannot overlook: the working class of Ireland is dying of hunger, and the landlords grow indignant and call for the help of the English police when the workers demonstrate their absurd revolutionary desire—to eat!

There is, for example, His Grace the Duke of Leicester —to quote no less sonorous name: his income from Ireland has increased to four hundred *contos*—and the unfortunate fellow has yet another two hundred *contos* more from more land of his in England. This nobleman, it is perhaps unnecessary to add, suffers neither hunger nor cold: on the other hand, the population of tenants who till his lands, and who by their sweat and labour wrest this income from their soil—their only solid acquisitions are hunger and cold. But this year they were colder and hungrier than usual: and they went in their rags, their feet bare in the snow, to beg His Grace, the Duke of Leicester, to make a ten per cent reduction in their rents —exaggerated, absurd and all-consuming as they are. His Grace replied (through his administrators, naturally: an English Duke never speaks personally to anyone other than another English Duke) that his circumstances did

73

not allow him to indulge in such liberality—and a repetition of such an entreaty would not be tolerated.

And His Grace's tenants turned back with heads bowed to face more cold and hunger.

I must say, incidentally, that if this request had been made by his tenants in England, instead of by his Irish ones, His Grace would have hastened to satisfy it most generously. This is because Ireland is a conquered country, and when the proletariat begins to complain, the police immediately grabs it by the collar: but in England, when the English labourer raises his leonine voice, the police stand motionless, Dukes turn pale, and the monarchic and feudal edifice trembles on its foundations.

But concerning His Grace the Duke of Leicester (let us enjoy his illustrious company as long as possible: *quand on prend du Duc on n'en saurait trop prendre*) let me tell you briefly what the agrarian relations are between a landlord and his tenant.

*

The soil belongs of course to the Lord. On what grounds I do not know; perhaps one of his great grand-mothers, more décolletée than usual one night, attracted the fickle eye of the charming Charles II, at one of those gallant evening gatherings during the Restoration: perhaps this fine property originated from that glance . . . The gay Stuart was so generous! And he had lived so poorly, so sadly, under the puritanical dictatorship of Cromwell! . . . And although Charles II had little money (the unfortunate fellow received an allowance from the King of France!) he had plenty of land in Ireland. Three leagues of pasture-land or arable ground, for a kiss and what went with it is not expensive by a Stuart's standards. And for a weak woman or her husband it is a magnificent business. Do, in Heaven's name, understand that I am making these suppositions about a theoretical Lord. Not all the sympathy I have for the Irish would lead me to suspect the chaste ladies of the House of Leicester . . .

As owner of the land, the Lord then leases it to the families who have lived there for years: the Irishman is deeply attached to the soil, as securely as a tree is by its roots, and will often prefer to die rather than abandon the barren strip of land which does not suffice to sustain him. The majority of Irish emigrants who go to America come mainly from the city labourers. Now, under the contract of the lease, the lessee is absolutely at the mercy of the landlord.

The price of the rents is purely arbitary. There is no scale of rents based upon the value of the land; there was something called Griffith's Irish Valuation Act, passed over thirty years ago by an agronomer of this name; but this valuation, just and favourable to the worker, is never accepted by the landlords. Here lies the origin of all Ireland's misery; rents, absurdly high, absorb all the income from the produce of the land, and the tenant can scarcely live, still less save.

Apart from the soil, the landlord must provide housing and tools of work: if there is no house on the land, or if it is in need of repair, the landlord will give his tenant some wood, a handful of nails, and a bundle of straw so that the tenant can put up a poor cabin, far inferior in comfort to the stables our cattle use; and to such a regal show of

75

generosity the landlord will perhaps add an old plough and a hoe. But these gifts are advances for which he charges two or three times their value, and which he makes the tenant pay for by quarterly instalments.

Surely one cannot act more generously and nobly.

Here, then, is the tenant, in possession of a roof, land and tools. It would seem that all he has to do now is begin tilling.

And so he would anywhere other than in Ireland. But Nature, fecund mother and mistress, behaves here worse even than the lords: if Nature had a place in the House of Lords she could not be harsher and more hostile to the poor tenants, and more miserly. Nature, to the Irish peasant, either comes in the form of stony soil or assumes the shape and texture of marshland.

The landlord offers him rocks on one side and a bog on the other, and then speaks with a mother's tenderness:

'Choose. From which side do you prefer to obtain your means of subsistence?'

What the poor peasant would prefer to do would be to get out of the place altogether: but as he would find the same sort of landlord wherever he went, and the same stony ground and the same bogland—he stays. And then the nobleman shows how generous he is once more. He is ready (because His Grace is kind-hearted) to drain the swamp, clear the land of stones, improve the soil. His Grace goes even further: His Grace (God reward him!) even offers him seed. And still more: His Grace (may the blessings of Heaven be on him!) gives him fertilizer too.

So here now is a happy tenant who has a house of his own and tools and seed and fertilizer . . . Only His Grace sets the prices which he thinks fit for the improvements made and the seed and fertilizers, and at the end of the year the rent, which was originally ten, has increased to twenty-five! As the land is poor and the winters terrible, the poor tenant cannot pay: so he goes to a money-lender —or to His Grace himself. And from that moment onwards he is entangled in a hopeless net of debts, IOU's, mortgaged harvests, accumulated interests, protests, the very devil—a mess from which he will never be able to extract himself. The result is a foregone conclusion: His Grace (through his agent) distrains his goods, seizes the grain that is in the granaries, the cattle which is in the pens, the small amount of linen in the chest, the wife's ear-rings, the pallets they lie on—and evicts him from his home and land—from the house that he himself built perhaps, from the land which he improved by his toil! Just like in the Middle Ages.

These evictions are the terror of the Irish. What can a poor wretch who suddenly finds himself, from one moment to the other, with wife and children and perhaps a crippled grandmother, out in the street, with winter howling around him and not a rag to cover him, not a crust of bread to eat, without house, or a future or hope? And note that this happens in areas—Ireland is a sparsely-populated country—where farmhouses are leagues apart.

This lack of neighbours makes evictions even more terrible. How many miles must they travel in rain or snow, with the children crying with hunger and the sick transported in a barrow, before they find a more fortunate farmer who has a corner of his hut to offer the vagrant family! And this for only a short time because all are poor, all are in debt, all threatened with eviction.

And all this while His Grace has his banquets, drinks his *Châteaux Margaux* at six *reis* a bottle, goes hunting, etc.—and lets the land from which he has evicted poor wretch Number One to tenant Number Two. Only Number Two, as the land is in better condition because of his predecessor, pays more: and after being exploited, overburdened with debts, drained dry, for two or three years, he is evicted too—to make way for Number Three. This unfortunate fellow goes through the same torments, *et sic per omnia.*

And the evictions are inevitable, because it is impossible for the tenant to pay the exorbitant rents and live.

This, you will understand, is only a vague outline of the situation, with only the chief characteristics. It is when one gets down to details that one sees the full horror of all the injustice and misery. But how can these things happen in the nineteenth century and right next door to the English people? How can so just a nation allow the existence of such an ignominious situation, you will ask. This was the question Victor Hugo put to Parnell, the leader of the Land League, in his famous interview a few days ago. And I shall answer with Parnell's words.

Such things do happen in the nineteenth century. And the English people were not aware of them. At least they were reported in such a way that instead of pity they aroused only anger.

And this is the fact. Ireland's misfortunes were made known through the voice of its agitators. But these men, since O'Connell, always made the mistake of mixing the complaints of the oppressed proletariat with the aspirations to national independence: so that England did not listen to the workers' demands because of the annoyance caused by the patriots' claims. The English people cannot bear the thought of Ireland's secession and the constitution of a republic: but it is ready to see that a just law of property be enforced.

The Fenians' mistake was to confuse the two issues—the national one and the agrarian: the wretched farmer appeared to English eyes in the guise of a rebel to the Union; and by unleashing hatred upon the two things, because they seemed identical ambitions, the voice begging for bread and the voice demanding autonomy were silenced indiscriminately.

And yet the English people instinctively felt that Ireland was suffering. A reform of the land laws was often proposed. But it was a vague appeal, with no unity of purpose: rather was it the expression of wounded sensibilities than the intimation of the nation's will.

So that the Members of Parliament, who come from the classes interested in keeping Ireland in her miscry, were content to make reforms in details, insignificant, imperceptible details, to satisfy the Englishman's compassion: and the old regime remained undisturbed as before. But it was sufficient for a few humanitarians to murmur with a sigh of relief: 'At last they are doing something for Ireland!' In actual fact nothing was being done.

The question of property, then, had to be separated from the question of independence: a legal movement had to be organized within the constitution with the exclusive purpose of stopping the landlords' abuses, and abolishing any idea of taking Ireland out of the United Kingdom. Then the English people, seeing the agrarian question in its full horror, isolated from other issues and in its proper proportions, detached from any rebellious demands and separatist agitations, would surely resolve to find a radical solution to these numerous wrongs of such long standing. This is what the Land League attempted to do.

This letter is long: and as I introduce this remarkable body, the Land League, I must do as the celebrated Ponson du Terrail did, when he introduced a new character, the providential hero, at the end of an instalment: defer the account of his exploits, his virtues and his beauty, and leave the reader in suspense until the next instalment. Bear in mind that we are at the point, in this our presentation of Irish History, when from the back of the stage the Land League, solemn and mysterious, suddenly steps forth.

Lord Beaconsfield

As I resume once more these *Letters from England*—which I could not write from Lisbon where I have been enjoying the idleness of Tityrus for a few months, *sub tegmine fagi*, in the shade of that pillar of Portuguese society that we call the *Gremio*—I must commemorate, although belatedly, the death of Benjamin Disraeli, Lord Beaconsfield, which occurred at dawn on May 19th at his house in Curzon Street in London. Lord Beaconsfield's illness—a complication of gout and asthma and bronchitis—dragged cruelly on for a long time; this, however, was eventually brought under control and what he in fact succumbed to was the weakness and weariness following seventy-seven years of a life so full of incident and excitement that Posterity will remember it as his greatest novel, far superior in style and interest to *Tancred* or *Endymion*.

From the first day Lord Beaconsfield lost all hope of recovering; but he looked death straight in the face as he always looked his political defeats in the face: with a cold disdainful courage and an air of easy superiority. During the illness, during the worst periods of pain, he responded with those brilliant and bitingly sarcastic remarks that

81

had always been his favourite retaliation when faced with a stronger adversary.

At nightfall on the 18th he gradually lapsed into a coma, and remained like that until dawn; a few moments before dying he stirred, then sat up, and even threw out his chest and raised his arms—as he used to do during the great debates in the House; then he fell back on his pillows, stretched out his hands to his secretaries, Lord Rowton and Lord Barrington, and murmured feebly: 'I am overcome!' and lay in his eternal sleep. And considering that, at that moment, all England, the whole world in fact, was waiting anxiously for news from that room in Curzon Street where a man lay breathing his last who, sixty years before, had been no more than an unknown young man working in a solicitor's office—one might say that after so happy a career, even his death was a happy one.

His funeral would have delighted his imagination—delighted certain delicate aspects of his artist's imagination. His will forbade a public funeral in Westminster Abbey—a strange attitude in a man who more than anything loved pomp and magnificent ceremonies: but then neither did he have the mournful trappings of death, the black crepe and black plumes, torches and mourning apparel and embroidered skulls—all this would have been most repugnant to his radiant spirit. He was buried in his beloved manor of Hughenden, among the trees of his park, one fresh spring morning, in the chapel decorated with flowers fit for wedding bells; the path he took was between jasmine and roses; instead of the tolling of the bells at Westminster he had the songs of his birds;

and the coffin, followed by the Princes of England, by all the ambassadors, by the aristocracy he had governed—was lost to sight beneath wreaths and sprays and bunches of primroses which Queen Victoria sent; they were, as she wrote in her own hand: 'The flowers he most loved.'

Then, the following day, in all the cathedrals throughout England, in every rustic chapel, the clergy extolled Lord Beaconsfield from the pulpit; in the universities and institutes and academies the professors commemorated that splendid career; on the platform at public meetings, at business conferences, wherever men were assembled together, voices were raised to honour his services and his brilliance; Lord Granville in the House of Lords, Gladstone in the House of Commons, solemnly made their public panegyrics; and for some days afterwards all the English papers, in fact the press of the whole civilized world (all except Portugal unfortunately) were full of his name, commemorating his books and his picturesque career.

And so Lord Beaconsfield disappeared—as had been his desire all his lifetime—amid a murmur of apotheosis.

And yet nothing appears less justified than such an apotheosis. Lord Beaconsfield was actually a statesman who wrote novels. Now his novels, as works of art, are beginning to appear to this scientific and analytical generation to be as false and artificial as the lyrical-religious novels of Viscount d'Arlincourt; and as a statesman Lord Beaconsfield cannot in any way be connected with any great progress in English society. To create the title of Empress of India for the Queen of England, to steal Cyprus, to restore certain prerogatives

of the Crown, to contrive the fiasco of Afghanistan—
these surely do not give him a claim to glory as a social
reformer. On the other hand, the writing of *Tancred* or
Endymion is not sufficient to set him apart in literature
when he had Dickens, Thackeray and George Eliot
among his contemporaries.

How is it, then, that England, such a practical and
level-headed country, let itself get carried away in a burst
of admiration for a man who was the personification, the
incarnation of all that is contrary to English temperament
and manners and taste? The fact is that Lord Beaconsfield, more than any other contemporary, caught the
Englishman's imagination—and in cold England, like
under warmer skies, the influence of the imagination is
very great.

One might at times laugh at his fantastic works of art
and protest against his theatrical political scheming, but
in spite of smiles and protests, his personality never
failed to be a source of admiration and fascination. Any
reasonably educated Englishman, if asked his opinion on
Lord Beaconsfield, would say: 'He was an extraordinary
man!'

Extraordinary—that is what he seems now that one
can view his life in its entirety, a life which seems not to
have been a natural product of facts and circumstances
but rather a subjective creation of his own will, like a
story springing from his own pen. Consider. He was born
a Jew—and became the leader of a Saxon-Norman
aristocracy, the proudest on earth; beginning in an
obscure literary circle and vegetating a while in a London
solicitor's office, he became the most famous Prime

Minister of a great empire; possessing only debts, he early became the inspiration behind great territorial fortunes; a man of imagination, of poetry and fantasy, he was the idol of the English middle classes, the most practical and utilitarian that have ever led a trading nation; with no religion nor moral code, he governed a Protestant country that cannot conceive of a possible social order outside its strict religion and its strict morality; confessing his contempt for all omnipotence of modern science, he was the greatest man of a society that wishes to give progress a purely scientific base; that is, he was English to the least possible extent, with an almost foreign way of being and feeling, and yet was for years and years the leader of England, the most hostile of countries to foreignness and a country, besides, which was well aware that it was not understood by the man who governed it. All this seems paradoxical—and the existence of Lord Beaconsfield was indeed a perpetual paradox in action. To achieve all this he had to be exceptional both in character and ability. And it is true that he was lacking in nothing as regards personal qualifications: he had a fantastically clever mind, an iron will, the serene courage of a hero, an inexhaustible vein of irony, a crepitating fire of eloquence, the absolute knowledge of men, brilliant penetration into the depths of character and temperament, a subtle power of persuasion, an irresistible personal charm—and all this contained (as in a luminous atmosphere) within a brilliance, a richness and impressiveness and unexpectedness that was, or effectively seemed to be, his own peculiar nature.

I shall begin by praising his appearance. They say he was as handsome as Apollo—and this was a great asset to his early triumphs; lately, in his old age, he was merely picturesque.

With his tall forehead, distinguished by those two extraordinary parallel curls falling over it, his glance, which was withdrawn, as if intent upon some deep private thoughts, that pure Israelite nose, the perpetually sarcastic curve of the mouth, the full, drooping lower lip, reminiscent of Mephistopheles—his was a physiognomy that one imagines will take its place in the gallery of history, serving future historians to explain a genius and a destiny. In his younger days, and when Fashion was sufficiently Romantic to allow it, he dressed in satins and velvets, and arrayed himself in medals and jewels, and even his trousers were embroidered in gold. Later his toilette became more discreet: he wore only those coats styled like a tunic which men of Jewish origin tend to wear, and his only ornament were the beautiful sprays which blossomed on his breast. One day during a political crisis, a French journalist found Lord Beaconsfield, a few moments before he was about to make a decisive speech in the House, engrossed in filling up with water the little crystal tube which was concealed behind his lapel to keep his roses fresh. This detail is characteristic of Lord Beaconsfield.

He was of Oriental origin and always had a love of pomp and jewellery and magnificent clothes; his novels abound in descriptions of palaces and banquets beside which the most sumptuous of Solomon's festivities are like the faded scenery of a fairground show; his style

86

suffers from this inclination: it is like a rich material, gold-embroidered, gem-adorned, heavy and glittering, falling in beautiful folds down the length of the idea. Money and gold always interested him, less for its social influence than for the mere splendour of its concentrated beauty. His heroes possess prodigious fortunes such as would be impossible to amass in the economic conditions of the modern world: Lothair, his famous Lothair, wishing to give a birthday present to a Catholic lady, offers her a cathedral made wholly of white marble, which he has had built and dedicated to her patron saint; its cost would surely have surpassed two thousand *contos*. We must confess that such a conception was *chic*. And Lothair gave this sort of present all the time. The banker Sidonia, one of Lord Beaconsfield's most curious creations, gave a letter of credit to his friend Tancred for the bankers of Syria, written in these terms: 'Pay the bearer on sight as much gold as would be needed to reconstruct in pure gold the four lions which adorn the right door of Solomon's temple.' Another very original idea.

I am sure that one of Lord Beaconsfield's greatest pleasures was the power of managing England's millions. All his ministries cost her copious rivers of gold—he spent gold like water—and he enjoyed the luxury, at England's expense, of putting into reality the epic liberality of his banker Sidonia. Even when he was in power, he was living a novel.

*

The outlines of his biography are well known. His father was one of those literary men, diligent and

87

mediocre, who spend their time groping in the dust of libraries and old folios, and collecting together whatever they find in literature or history that is quaint and curious.

Benjamin Disraeli was therefore born amid books— literally amid books, for the house in which the Disraelis lived was minuscule, and in the child's room there was space only for a chair and a cradle among the accumulation of ancient tomes. Disraeli senior was a Jew: but fortunately for the future destiny of his son he broke with the synagogue and all the Disraelis were Christians. Benjamin was seventeen years old at the time, and at his baptism his godfather was a certain Samuel Rogers, famous for being one of the richest bankers in the City and one of the most elegiac poets of his time—and famous, moreover, for not featuring in history either as a banker or as a poet but simply as a most refined *gourmet*, the great Lucullus of London, who gave the finest and most celebrated dinners in Europe.

Thus marked with the Christian label, Benjamin Disraeli set off into the great world, but very shortly landed in a solicitor's office, where it is said that this proud youth, who even then considered himself a god, stayed for two years, drawing up wills and procurations. With that same pen, however, he was also writing *Vivian Grey*: and his great career dates from the fantastic sensation that this novel produced. This work, excepting a few fleeting flashes of a yet uncertain talent, is, on the whole, heavy and somewhat vague; but it satisfied the current taste for scandal and intrigue, featuring as it did all the outstanding personalities of London society—politicians, dandies, reigning queens of fashion, poets, speculators.

88

The best result of *Vivian Grey* was to make Disraeli junior (as he signed himself) the favourite of Lady Blessington and Count d'Orsay, the two major figures in London at that time, who had the most select, most intelligent, most sought-after *salon* in all English society.

These two together formed a type destined to reign. Lady Blessington was a woman of gracious and Olympian beauty, with an extremely forthright character and highly stimulating mind. The Count d'Orsay was the man who for twenty years ruled fashion and taste and manners with the same undisputed authority as Bismarck today arbitrates in Europe.

To adopt a fashion in ties or admire a poet who had not been approved by the Count d'Orsay was to run a risk similar to that of a nation that today organizes a military expedition without the tacit authorization of Prince Bismarck. Lady Blessington, among other embarrassing things, had a daughter: the handsome d'Orsay, goodness knows why—he never knew himself—wed this young lady. The young couple went to live with Lady Blessington; and very soon, what with her brilliant husband and her glittering mother, the poor Countess d'Orsay began to look like a dim lamp flickering between two stars. She then did a most sensible and spirited thing: she went out altogether, and disappeared. And the Count d'Orsay and Lady Blessington, freed of that young lady who had saddened and frozen the atmosphere of their drawing-room with her cold, honest air—now began to shine more tranquilly, like close constellations in the social firmament of London. And London bowed before this new and original domestic situation, as it bowed before a new overcoat of the Count's, or before a literary decision of Lady Blessington's.

Benjamin Disraeli soon became one of the heroes of this *salon*—where he exhibited from the beginning that air of tranquil superiority, of correct disdain, that was one of the secrets of his strength. Generally he remained silent, leaning against the marble mantlepiece and adopting the pose of a melancholy Apollo, abandoning himself to the caressing glances of the ladies, who saw in him the radiant incarnation of the poetic Vivian Grey. His most intimate friends, beginning with Lady Blessington, already called him Vivian, *dear Vivian*. The Count d'Orsay did a portrait of him—an honour which he rarely gave, and the most highly esteemed in this curious world.

All these triumphs of Disraeli junior could not fail to surprise Disraeli senior. One day, when someone was telling him that his son was writing a novel in which featured dukes and all sorts of great men, this old and diligent man of letters exclaimed: 'Dukes, gentlemen! But my son has never even set eyes on one!'

He saw many after that, he saw all of them—and governed them all with a rod of iron. But at this time Disraeli junior was still a radical, or at least he adopted this attitude. He was even contemplating his *Revolutionary Epick*, his only work in verse, a vague rhapsody which I have never read but which the most benevolent critics consider a volume of two hundred pages, not one line of which is tolerable. And it is a curious thing that so distinguished a man, sceptical and experienced as he was, never lost the almost comic naivety of considering himself as great a poet as Virgil or Dante, and the fantastic expectation that future generations would put the *Revolutionary Epick* on a level with the *Aeneid* or the *Divine Comedy*.

In spite of being an abominable poet and a perfect dandy—or perhaps because of this—Benjamin Disraeli was known at this time as one of the leaders of the movement called *Young England*.

Young England consisted of a group of aristocratic and ardent young men who were steeped in revolution through literature; they talked about Humanity and wanted more than anything else to find a Rotten Borough which would elect them Members of Parliament; they cultivated Platonic love in the *salons* and wished to see the people happy—as long as it was they who were in power to promote this happiness, and (a telling characteristic of their manners and pose) when they wrote to one another they addressed each other as 'darling'.

They had other characteristics: they wore their hair like Nazarites; they had the courage (outstanding at that time) to admire the detested Byron; and they tried to raise the standard of cookery in England!

In the meantime Benjamin Disraeli was already decided upon throwing off his radicalism the moment it seemed necessary to the interests of his career. And, poor and unknown though he was, he could see this future career of his as clear and triumphant as if he had it before his eyes, written down step by step as in a programme.

While the Tories were at the height of their power, his reply to Lord Melbourne, then Prime Minister, was characteristic when this gentleman asked him what he wanted to be, 'I want shortly to become Prime Minister,' answered the dandy with his haughty Vivian Grey air.

Lord Melbourne considered such a reply mere insolent bragging. And so it seemed some time later when Disraeli, now Member for Wycombe, made his maiden speech—and found his voice drowned by laughter and cat-calls. As he was unable to control the tumult he stopped speaking, and merely said:

'I sit down now, but the time will come when you *will* hear me.'

And the time came when not only the House of Commons but all England, all the Continent, all the civilized earth, listened anxiously to the words which fell from his lips, and which brought with them either peace or war in Europe.

2

The drawing-room reputation which Lord Beaconsfield enjoyed took some time to turn into popularity; but his popularity, when it did come, penetrated swiftly to the enormous working class, and in a few years it had become the resounding reputation that made his name almost a household word in every part of the English-speaking world—in the poorest fishing village in Cornwall, in the Australian bush, among the wild hill-folk in the Highlands—a reputation that even made the Germans flock to the railway stations to see the 'great Englishman' when he went to the Berlin Congress. And this recognition of glory constitutes one of the most curious phenomena of Lord Beaconsfield's career; for one does not generally appreciate the outstanding difficulty there is in obtaining a reputation, even a mediocre one.

There is nothing so illusory as the extent of fame; at times it seems as if a reputation must be known to the edges of a kingdom—when actually it scarcely passes the last houses of one's quarter. When Alexandre Dumas, Père, was at the height of his fame, he was amazed that the magistrate of a town on the outskirts of Paris—an educated man, moreover—did not know how to spell the glorious name of Dumas!

And if we could reduce to numbers the sizes of contemporary reputations, we should be horrified to discover how paltry were the results. We journalists and critics and artists and literary-minded men consider it almost impossible that there is someone in Europe who has not read Victor Hugo, or who has not at least heard of this simply-pronounced name, which for half a century has assailed, and most vigorously, the human ear; however, outside France possibly no more than five thousand people will have read Victor Hugo—and no more than ten thousand, surely, the number of people who have heard of him, even including the vast democratic mass of which he is the official chronicler. And even this is fantastic progress—since the time when Voltaire's ambition was to have *a hundred readers*!

The well-known allegory of Fame, with its hundred voices, lauding the name of a man, and flying from one end of the Universe to the other, is one of the most shamelessly false images which Antiquity has left us! This thundering of a hundred trumpets dies out like a sigh in the modest area of a gossipping society or a coterie: and nothing travels slower than Fame. A parcel of cloth will take four days to reach Lisbon from London—and the names of Tennyson, Browning, Swinburne, the three great poets of England who for forty years have been her pride and glory, still have not reached Lisbon. It is true that all the world needs flannel—and not all the world loves poetry.

But a celebrity can have difficulty not only in crossing frontiers—he may find it especially difficult, at times even impossible, to gain the attention of the great host of his fellow citizens. This is especially so in a country like England, where the bitter struggle for existence, the pre-occupation with the daily bread, the fierce competition, does not leave time for idle moments such as the Spaniards and Portuguese enjoy, when they lie on their backs, basking in the sun, ready to watch and admire the feeblest firework that lights up the sky.

In England the Duke of Wellington was undoubtedly popular because he won the Battle of Waterloo, and therefore, according to popular belief, saved England from invasion. Gladstone is known in a hundred cities and a thousand villages, because he lightened the nation of its heavy tax burden. But these are the exceptions: other English celebrities, whether they are politicians like Lord Salisbury or philosophers like Spencer, or poets like Browning, or artists like Herkomer, remain completely ignored by the great majority. Theirs are reputations contained within the drawing room, or academy or club or newspaper office.

Now Lord Beaconsfield never really did anything to become so popular and well-remembered; his name was connected with no great institution, with no great public charity, with no victorious campaign. On the contrary,

94

everything in his basic personality seemed to destine him to unpopularity: his origin, his anti-English gestures and habits, his sarcastic vein, his flowery, subtle oratory, the sheer artificiality of his literary conceptions, and certain very marked aspects of his Semitic background. Added to this, he represented to the great majority of the nation a *parvenu* of oligarchical authority, blindly hostile to the idea of democracy and popular government.

His astounding popularity seems to me to spring from two causes: the first was his idea (which inspired all his political thinking) that England should become the dominant power in the world, a type of Roman Empire, constantly enlarging its colonies, taking possession of the uncivilized continents and 'Anglicizing' them, reigning in every market, deciding by the strength of its sword the question of war or peace in all parts of the world, imposing its institutions, its language, its customs, its art— he dreamed of a globe made up of land and ocean exclusively British, whirling regularly through space.

This ideal, which took the name of imperialism in the glorious days of Lord Beaconsfield, is a cherished idea of every Englishman: the same liberal newspapers that denounced the dangers of this Roman-type policy with such fury, enjoyed, in their hearts, immense satisfaction and pride in the very act of condemning it as inappropriate. There was as much arrogance in condemning such an Empire as in conceiving it, and in saying, with an air of noble renunciation: 'We do not want the responsibility of governing the world!'

Lord Beaconsfield, being the official incarnation of this imperial idea, naturally became as popular as the idea.

He was considered the instrument of England's external grandeur, the man who made her the feared ruler, who kept John Bull's sword raised and gleaming in the eyes of the world. Gladstone, Bright, the great liberal school, known as the Manchester School, was now accused of being, because of its policy of abstention, interested only in material betterment, in the improvement of finances and domestic affairs—leaving English prestige in Europe to die out.

And now along came this extraordinary Jew, backed by the wealth and the domestic prosperity which the liberals had bequeathed him, to place England at the head of all nations once more, so that the lion's roar should resound the length and breadth of the globe . . .

The whole country was swollen for years with this grand arrogance, which Lord Beaconsfield was always encouraging with his bellicose speeches, his theatrical threats, the concentrations of fleets, a constant movement of regiments, invasions here and there, the occupation of Cyprus, what amounted to almost an appropriation of the isthmus of Suez—always some brilliant move so that England stepped out from the midst of his rhetorical fireworks in the guise of the queen of the earth. And John Bull loved this, although he could see that England's sword, after flashing for a moment in the air, was invariably thrust back into its sheath; although he understood that money was being spent like spring water; although he realized that taxes were increasing; although he saw that England was taking upon herself responsibilities out of proportion to her strength.

Then one day England's great practical sense saw

clearly that she must shine less in the eyes of the world—
and busy herself more with the internal machine which
was in need of repair: and she dismissed the grand Lord
Beaconsfield and called the practical Gladstone—the man
who put her finances in order again and lessened the tax
burden and made great national reforms . . . But in spite
of all this, Beaconsfield remained as the type of statesman who, more than anyone else, loved and desired the
imperial grandeur of his motherland.

To this reason for his popularity must be added another
—propaganda. Never did any other statesman have such
propaganda, never so continuous nor in such proportions,
nor so expert. The major newspapers of England, Germany and Austria, and even France, are (no one would
deny it) in the hands of Israelites. Now the Jewish world
has never failed to consider Lord Beaconsfield a Jew—in
spite of the drops of Christian water which moistened his
head. This insignificant incident never prevented Lord
Beaconsfield from celebrating in his works and imposing
by his own personality, the superiority of the Jewish race
—and on the other hand never hindered European
Jewry from affording him the tremendous support of its
gold, its plotting and its publicity. When he was young it
was Jewish money that paid his debts; later it is Jewish
influence which gives him his first seat in Parliament; it
is the Jewish heritage which blesses the success of his
first government; finally, it is the press in the hands of
Jews, the telegraph system in the hands of Jews, which
constantly praise him, extol his ability as a statesman, as
an orator, as a writer, as a hero, as a genius!

As a novelist, Lord Beaconsfield never really wrote a novel in the modern sense of the word. Some of his novels are pamphlets in which the characters constitute living arguments, conquering or being defeated not only according to the logic of their temperaments and the demands of the plot, but also according to the needs of the controversy or thesis. Others are pure allegories, like those in decorative paintings on the walls of public monuments. In one of the most celebrated, *Lothair*, there is an ideal youth, the incarnation of the English spirit, who loves three women successively: an Italian, married to an American—a beautiful creature she is, with a classic profile and the figure of a goddess, who represents Democracy; an ardent young lady with unruly black hair, who is always in a state of ecstasy, and is the personification of the Catholic Church; and finally, a sweet fair maiden, serious, grave and tender, who symbolizes Protestantism. After hesitating among these three passions, he decides, like a good Englishman, to marry Protestantism, I mean, the fair maiden, retaining a secret affection for Democracy, I mean for the superb American with the marble profile. Moral: the happiness of a people lies in its possession of strong Christian principles, allied to a moderate enjoyment of liberty. This would make a splendid fresco in Parliament. And Lord Beaconsfield accentuated the allegorical details with such ingenuity that it makes one smile at times: the American, for example, that is, Democracy, always appears at *soirées* and parties dressed in Greek fashion, with a star of brilliants upon her forehead, like the head of the Republic on the French five-franc coins!

The novels always take place in a fairy-tale atmosphere: as I said before, everything happens in fabulous palaces in sombre luxury, there are parties such as the Medicis never dreamed of, and bankers' and dukes' fortunes in comparison with which the Croesuses, the Monte-Cristos, the Rothschilds, all the wealthy men of legend and reality, appear like despicable beggars.

The language of these characters corresponds to the splendour of their residences and to the nebulous sphere of their destinies. Young maidens of eighteen years, prosaically living in Belgrave Square, speak to their young men with the allegorical pomp of the *Song of Songs*; and when (as frequently happens) two brilliant souls like Sidonia or Mrs Coningsby converse, one can see, flitting swiftly from lip to lip, the shining images and the glittering conceits as if the two creatures were reciting to each other numbers from *Intermezzo* or Petrarch's sonnets.

This language, moreover, fits the ideas and sentiments and adventures that he attributes to his protagonists; anything real and human is left strictly outside his transcendental creations: speaking like poets, they naturally behave like chimeras.

His most famous hero, Tancred, goes to Jerusalem and Syria for this purpose: *to penetrate the Asiatic mystery*. You do not understand? Simple: as Jerusalem and the plains of Syria are the only place in the Universe where God has spoken to Man, the only place where prophets and Messiahs appear, where the New Laws have emerged from the murmur of the rivers and from the echoes of the deserts—the New Laws which have given humanity new destinies—the young Tancred sets off so that there, in those parts, God might speak to him, a ray of light might illuminate him, a religion might be revealed to him, and having set out from London as a simple Lord, he might return to Regent Street as the Messiah and regenerator of societies!

And what happens to Tancred in Syria, you might ask? The same thing that happens to all Lord Beaconsfield's characters, who in the first pages set off for superhuman destinies, like the old knights of the Round Table: they marry a nice pretty girl and have numerous offspring amid much happiness . . .

And the Asiatic mystery? It seems he could not find it. But he discovered strange things and rare: for example a pagan people where a beautiful priestess of Apollo reigns who still, in modern times, celebrates noble Hellenic forms of worship, and falls in love with Tancred. But Tancred, being a Christian gentleman, after defending her from the invasion of another people who worship infamous idols, runs off, runs off full speed, leaving the classic queen to sob with love at the feet of the statue of Astarté. After that he is almost made King of Libya. All in all, a splendid, brilliant confusion. And all this takes place about 1855, at the time of the Paris Exhibition.

But what a marvellous talent, what art, what abundance of imagination, to set out in all its brilliance this disordered monument of Idealism!

*

What a skilful artist, in fact, and how powerful he is at times!

In spite of the extravagant artifice of his fiction, in spite of the vague and at the same time mannered style of his conceptions, of the plots and the characters which at times mystify—his novels never fail to hold one's interest, never fail, I must admit, to captivate. We always feel a sincere enthusiasm, in which one senses the poetic love with which he follows his generous heroes and his beautiful women along their unreal destinies. Then his exquisite sensitivity, his somewhat conventional but nevertheless spirited idealism—the touches of a most refined taste— lead him to endow his characters and the action in which they move with so spiritual a beauty, such nobility of manners, that one lifts one's eyes from the pages and one's imagination is captivated by this fictitious world, this poetic humanity, where nothing low or coarse exists and where the most marvellous, transcendental forms of thought and feeling and living shine out brilliantly.

This gives him a quality of enchantment, a radiance. Characters, landscapes, interiors, the very movement of the adventure—all this is bathed in a serene, graceful light. Portraying things as he did outside social reality, and not having to present the sombre shadows, he could exclude from his vast paintings all that is hard in life, all that is brutal and ugly and evil and stupid—all the various forms of human baseness.

He wrote for a wealthy society, a noble, literary and refined society, and he showed them a world of crystal and gold, spinning round in a beautiful harmony, bathed in rosy hues.

*

I have insisted on this unreal aspect of Lord Beaconsfield's books. However, a man like this, a former dandy, a
critic and a statesman accustomed to governing, an
observer by necessity, could not help but accumulate a
large experience of characters and society; and this
experience would naturally have emerged in his portraits
of life. And there it is in fact; amid the great symbolical
creations of an imagination run riot (Tancred, Lothair,
Sibyl), a very real world moves, sketched in bold, accurate
strokes, figures of flesh and blood represented with
singular vividness in design and colour. They are the
secondary characters, his politicians, his plotters, his men-
of-letters, his fashionable women, his elegant lords. All
these types were copied from the originals. London knew
them, and straightway named them; and the scandal of
these portraits was one of the very causes of Lord
Beaconsfield's success. But even for readers who do not
frequent London society, and do not know the originals,
these characters are interesting—because they are alive.

Generally they are merely sketches, but masterly ones;
and appearing as they do, standing out as they do, beside
pure creations of the imagination, unreservedly poetic
and of hazy outline, these real people make a sharper
impact, like the profiles of real humanity, emerging from
a mist of mythology.

These are the ones that really capture one's interest,
and out of the vast gallery of Lord Beaconsfield's creations it is they who will be remembered.

It would be impossible in this brief profile, made up
merely of impressions, to set down all the characteristics of
an individuality as complex as that of Lord Beaconsfield.

Few men can have produced so curious a conflict of opinions: some say he was a great statesman, others that he was a charlatan; critics have painted him both as a talented novelist—and as a poor weaver of unreal tales! A party man, he suffered, both in politics and literature, idolatry from one quarter and rancour from the other. One thing, however, he had in his favour: everyone who was mediocre hated him.

It is difficult to separate the politician from the novelist in him: he always included his politics in his works of art, which thus became resounding manifestos of his ideas as a statesman—and he acted out novels while in government which often seemed like the background for a drama, with him sitting there, pen in hand, working out the most effective moves. Whatever he was, England lost one of its most picturesque and original talents in Lord Beaconsfield.

In his personal life he was a happy man. As a young man he sketched out the plan of his future life, as one might prepare a plot for a novel, and he carried it out to the fullest extent, in every aspect, in a continuous series of triumphs. He was handsome, he was loved, he was rich, he had the best wife in England (so he said), he left a vast literary opus, he was the chosen confidant of his Queen, he governed his land, took an important hand in the destinies of the world, and ended his life in an apotheosis. Was he then absolutely happy? No, this triumphant man lived with a secret, a small, absurd disadvantage: his French was far from fluent!

The English in Egypt

I

UNTIL FIVE WEEKS ago Alexandria could have been described in the inviting style of the tourist guides as a rich city with a population of 250,000 Europeans and Arabs, lively, enterprising and prosperous, and rapidly becoming an Eastern Marseilles. But no guide, however flattering it might be, could call it interesting.

In spite of having survived two thousand years, and of having been, after Athens and Rome, the greatest centre of luxury, letters and trade which ever flourished in the Mediterranean, Ptolemy's ancient city did not possess a single monument of its past except for a column, now standing beside an old Moslem cemetery, erected in former days by a Roman prefect in honour of Diocletian, a column known by the singular title of Pompey's Pillar; and further off, lying in the sand, a Pharaonic obelisk of the Temple of Luxor, which enjoyed the grotesque nickname of Cleopatra's Needle. And even this relic now rests in London on the Thames Embankment, standing on a bronze pedestal illuminated by electric light and deafened by the roar of trains.

The European quarters of Alexandria are of fairly recent origin. (Fifty years ago, before Mohammed-Ali put in hand its reconstruction, the great metropolis which struck awe into the heart of the Caliph Omar had dwindled to a village making its living from fishing and a small trade in sponges.) They comprise a vast square— the famous Consuls' Square, the pride of all the Levant —and wide streets with French names, French stucco on the façades, French names on the shops, French cafés, French brothels—just like a *faubourg* of Bordeaux or Marseilles, transported to Egypt and adorned here and there with palm trees.

The Arab part of the city had no Oriental picturesqueness about it: there were merely streets running almost straight, with humble whitewashed terrace-roofed houses, built of a single storey in a compound of mud and sand, which the slightest sea-breeze would scatter in clouds.

An ugly city, shabby, unhealthy, evil-smelling, Alexandria was a place to be visited rapidly, viewed from a swift-moving carriage; and it was swiftly erased from the memory, as soon as the Cairo-bound train left the station, and from among the first crops of the Delta, along the canals, the white ibis could be seen no more—the oldest inhabitants of Egypt, formerly gods and even today considered sacred birds.

Such, however, was Alexandria: its bay was filled with steam-packets and freighters and warships; its docks crowded with vociferating, uniformed humanity; its great hotels, its flags fluttering over the consulates, its enormous warehouses, its hundreds of open carriages, its thousand and one music-halls and brothels; its streets where the Egyptian soldiers in their white linen uniforms walked arm in arm with the seamen of Marseilles and Liverpool, where the camel-trains, led by a Bedouin with a lance at his shoulder, obstructed the American trams, where the green-turbaned sheiks, on their white donkeys, trotted past businessmen in their French landaus driven by coachmen in livery. Such was Alexandria, the world's most perfect example of a Levantine city; and, beneath its deep blue sky, it did not cut a bad figure as the business capital of Egypt, a Mediterranean Liverpool.

This was the state of affairs five or six weeks ago. Today, at the moment of writing, Alexandria is no more than an enormous pile of ruins.

Of the European district and the famous Consuls' Square, and its hotels and banks and offices and café-brothels, only a disorderly rubbish heap remains, with here and there a blackened wall threatening to fall.

For the fourth time in history, Alexandria has ceased to exist.

Considering that this is Egypt, the land of ancient curses, one might think, in the presence of such a catastrophe, that Jehovah's wrath was the cause—one of those fits of wrath from which the pages of the Bible still tremble, when the One True God, seeing a city consumed with the black stain of sin, leapt from the clouds and cauterized it with fire, as if it were an open sore eating into the Earth. But this time it was not Jehovah. It was simply the English Admiral Sir Beauchamp Seymour, in England's name, and under the orders of Mr Gladstone's liberal government, solemnly and methodically deploying his eighty-ton naval guns.

It would perhaps be dishonest, certainly dispropor-
tionate, to add to the names of the great men who have in
the last two thousand years attacked Alexandria and left
her in ruins—to the names of Caracalla the pagan, Cyril
the saint, Diocletian the persecutor, Ben-Amon the
bloodthirsty—the name of Mr William Gladstone, the
humanitarian, paladin of tyrannized nations, apostle of
Christian democracy. But if, on the one hand, Mr Gladstone's policy is evidently not a result of pure personal
ferocity, as was Caracalla's, who laid waste Alexandria
because a literary-minded poet of that city attacked him
in an epigram, this sudden aggression by a fleet of twelve
battleships, iron strongholds floating upon the waters,
against the decrepit fortifications of Mohammed-Ali,
this bombardment of an Egyptian city, while England was
at peace with Egypt, seems extraordinarily similar to the
primitive policy of Caliph Omar or the Persian Emperors,
which consisted of this: be strong, fall upon the weak,
destroy lives and seize property. Which shows that what
is here called 'England's imperial policy', or 'England's
interests in the East', can lead a Christian statesman to
repeat the crimes of a Moslem pirate, and Mr Gladstone,
who is almost a saint, to behave more or less like Ben-
Amon, who was a complete monster. Better not to have
been Prime Minister of England! And that was what
John Bright thought, for rather than be an accomplice to
this brutal destruction of an inoffensive city, he handed in
his resignation to the Cabinet, left friends of fifty years'
standing, and went modestly to take up his old place on
the Opposition benches.

Everything immediately connected with the annihilation

107

of Alexandria can be simply told, especially if one confines oneself to the broad outline, which is all that can interest anyone who is morally and materially three thousand leagues away from Egypt and its misfortunes.

At the beginning of last June, the English Admiral Sir Beauchamp Seymour found himself in the waters of Alexandria, commanding a strong fleet with a French squadron anchored alongside, flying Admiral Conrad's ensign. France and England were there with guns primed, companionably watching over Alexandria, just as for the last two years in Cairo they have been companionably inspecting the Egyptian economy: for they surely know that if Egypt (in debt up to the tops of the pyramids with the financial bourgeoisie of Paris and London) should fail to pay her instalments, France and England, maternally protecting the interests of their money-lenders, would instal two gentlemen in Cairo—Messrs. Coloin and Blegnières—both with the office of secretaries in the Egyptian Treasury, both of them charged with collecting the revenue, administering it, and applying the most profitable part to the repayment of principle and interest on the famous Egyptian debt!

Thus the two flags of England and France were really two enormous credit notes, hoisted to the mastheads of the battleships. The two bourgeois gentlemen, Coloin and Blegnières, made a further appearance in the persons of Admiral Seymour and Admiral Conrad. And in the Bay of Alexandria, opposite Egypt, one of the greatest bankrupts of the East, the united fleets of the two most advanced civilizations of the West represented nothing other than armed usury.

This is the real state of affairs. Officially the battle-ships were carrying out manoeuvres there, but in actual fact it amounted to a foreign intervention, because incidents had been occurring in Egypt and the Khedive had declared himself 'under duress'. All those who know the contemporary history of Portugal and other curious constitutional countries, know what is meant by this delightful phrase, 'The King is under duress!' It means that His Majesty is in his palace surrounded by a menacing populace which has snatched up sticks and stuck a flag on the end of one and come to impose this exceptionally disagreeable formula upon the King: decrease of royal authority and increase of public liberty.

If the King has a few faithful regiments stationed behind the palace, he puts on his general's uniform at this point and has his people put to the sword; if, however, the soldiers are unfortunately on the side of the citizens, then the King declares himself 'under duress' and asks a neighbouring King, a stronger and less embarrassed King, to send a division to restore order—that is, to preserve for the King all his royal authority, dispersing the attempt at public liberty with bullets. This, nowadays, does not happen in Europe, but in the East it appears to be a most proper method of calming national disturbances.

The Khedive, that most excellent and peaceful youth, had been the victim of a *pronunciamento* planned in the Spanish way, but put into action in the Turkish manner. A Colonel, Arabi Bey, who was shortly to become Arabi Pasha, presented himself with a number of other officers at the palace, and after a low bow, which in Turkish etiquette involves devotedly kissing the Khedive's coat, as we in Lisbon kiss St Anthony's robe, reminded His Highness of the need to carry out reforms, some of them purely military and for the Colonel's benefit, others political, to the advantage of the large Fellahin population, and so wide in their application that they constituted a change of regime. His Highness listened, murmured those phrases about love of his nation, the happiness of his subjects, etc., that ceremony dictates on the occasion of royal bewilderment and seemed so pleased with the interest that these officers were taking in the prosperity of the Nile Valley, that he rewarded them in oriental style— by inviting them to a banquet. Spirits were high around the festive table, champagne bubbled, contrary to the prescriptions of the *Koran*, and Egypt's future, amid the taste of truffles and the perfume of flowers, looked rosy. Coffee was served in the gardens: and while servants were entering from one side with liqueurs, the police appeared from the other with handcuffs. Arabi and his comrades, the last cigars His Highness had offered them still between their lips, were led to their pallets in a prison cell.

There can be nothing more delightful—nor more Turkish.

All Europe, which admires energy, enthusiastically applauded His Highness's spirit!

2

ARABI'S REVENGE—REFORMERS AND COLONELS—
THE FELLAHIN PROGRAMME—THE CONFERENCE
OF CONSTANTINOPLE—THE GRAND TURK'S
CONFUSION—THE SQUADRONS

The Khedive had a few calm days of triumph after this.
When he opened his *Times* or his *Journal des Débats*
(for this is a cultured prince), he could rejoice, as he
perceived that these two powerful organs of European
opinion considered him an energetic potentate, full of the
vigour befitting a descendant of the great Mohammed-
Ali, intensely jealous of his rights and able to maintain
order in his states with a rod of iron—worthy, in fact, of
the respect of the Great Powers.

One morning, however, the palace was surrounded by
troops—twelve thousand men with eighteen pieces of
artillery—beseeching His Highness to release Arabi and
appoint him Minister of War. And they gave this reason,
which was plain enough according to Arab logic: as the
army approved Arabi Bey's reforms, they felt that he
would carry them out far more comfortably seated in the
Minister of War's armchair rather than lying on his hard
prison bed.

The Khedive, who had perhaps just finished savouring
a further glorification of his energy in the *Times*, agreed,
and even went so far as to declare that he had always respected Arabi. There and then Arabi, on bended knee,
was given the title Pasha, and Arabi Pasha went from gaol
to power to the sound of military bands.

In such circumstances a European leader will launch his programme as high into the firmament of progress as the fireworks that explode during the celebrations, and with no less din and glitter—and generally, like the fireworks, only a burnt-out stub will remain. And we are so accustomed to this, in these privileged regions here, where the train whistle is a familiar sound, that discerning journals began to mistrust Arabi when they did not see him go forward with his programme in hand. He did not have one.

In a Moslem country, under the writ of the *Koran*, there are none: furthermore, it was not to be expected that an Egyptian soldier (as M. Gambetta remarked with clumsy, needless irony) should stumble upon the unpublished principles of the Revolution of '89 in the tombs of the Pharaohs. By no means. But Arabi did have three or four ideas which, had Europe been decent enough to let him carry them out, could have been the beginning of a new Egypt, an Egypt belonging to itself, governing itself, an *Egypt for the Egyptians*, not a race of slaves bound to the family of Mohammed-Ali, still less a free eating-house for starving Europeans.

As I see it, what prevented Arabi from becoming a reformer was his being a Fellah colonel, son of a Fellah, born in one of those miserable villages—heaps of huts made of dried mud which blacken the length of the Nile. Having lived in the abject misery of the Fellahin—the worst that exists on the face of the earth—he, more than anyone, had the right to stand up in the name of the long years of oppression suffered by the Fellahin. But at the same time Arabi was a soldier who had earned his promotions in the lengthy stretches of duty in the garrisons of Upper Egypt and in the campaigns in the Sudan; he had returned from these with all the pride of his career and all the pedantry of the sabre: not only had he the prowess of a good soldier but he had a soldier's weaknesses, and was therefore ready, as soon as his voice carried weight, to put it to the service of his fellow soldiers' demands. He represented, by origin and profession, the two great classes of the Egyptian people—the soldier and the Fellah; and from the moment in which the self-seeking, the greedy and the oppressed came upon the scene, he appeared to be the only man in Egypt willing to risk prison or exile for his ideas. He rapidly became, naturally enough, the leader of the popular party which wanted sweeping national reforms, and also head of the military party which desired only benefits for the army. Thus in Arabi patriotism was unfortunately mingled with insubordination.

In his reforms there was an unhealthy mixture of far-reaching liberal ideas, vindicating the rights of the worker, and the most specious demands from the barracks, revealing a rebellious soldier. With the same enthusiasm, and as if the two things were of equal value in the task of regenerating Egypt, he requested a parliamentary constitution and an increase in pay and promotion for his fellow colonels. What happened? Those in Europe who wanted to see the Khedive's regime continue (a financial enterprise which gave large dividends) made such a fuss at the troops' scandalous pretensions that the just demands of the people could not be heard and Arabi was easily discredited, his good patriotic side being hidden and his bad side, that of a turbulent colonel, being accentuated.

Any revolution directed by colonels is justly suspect to our modern European spirit; but Arabi is an Egyptian; and in Egypt, where the Fellahin, although they are as intelligent as any of our working-classes, are little more than an irresponsible horde of slaves, and where the army constitutes the cultured class—any work of progress must necessarily be carried out by the soldier. Europe, however, is unaware of this, or rather, it pretends to be. The demands of the guard-house put the claims of the humble labourer in the shade—and Arabi lost the authority he might have had in Europe as leader of the Fellahin, for he spoke with a sword in his hand amid a crowd of soldiers.

Certainly Arabi is no Mazzini, no Louis Blanc. He is an Arab of the old type, who has read only one book—the *Koran*. But as a man he possessed qualities of heart and courage and intelligence that even those who were fighting him so brutally dared not deny. And as a patriot he enjoys the stature of the great patriots: there were surely many Egyptians in Egypt who loathed the Khedive's regime and resented the sight of their rich valley of the Nile being devoured by foreigners, as in former days it had been laid waste by locusts: but these resigned themselves to bowing their shoulders and invoking the name of Allah.

This man is the first who understood that Allah, although so great and strong, could not attend to everything and so decided to take up his sword in the name of the Fellah, against the allied oppression of the Turkish Pashas and the Christian money-lenders.

And what were, after all, the reforms of Arabi, this monster of sedition?

Arabi wanted, in the first place, to put an end to the Khedive's absolute authority, and see Egypt governed by an elected Assembly; and, in keeping with this new regime, he wanted a radical reform in the use of public money, which up till then had been allocated, part to the Khedive's court, part to the harem of the Sultan who was the suzerain of Egypt, part to the closed ranks of foreign civil servants, and a large part to pay off the debts in Paris and London; this left so little for the needs of the country that for two years the army had received hardly any pay!

Arabi did not deny this foreign debt, contracted by that splendid spendthrift, Ismail Pasha, but recognized by the nation which felt honour-bound to pay it: he merely did not agree that France and England should be installed in Cairo, their noses in the Treasury, waiting for the taxes to fall due so as to seize the lion's share; so that in order to satisfy the voracity of his European creditors the Fellah was crushed with taxes, so much so that, however much he sweated day and night, he had eventually to resort to the European usurer. Strange! Europe appeared officially as creditor and, in order to get paid, secretly supplied a money-lender!

But Arabi's reforms reached a crucial point when they touched upon the situation of the foreigners in Egypt. There were monstrous pretensions here. Arabi demanded that the privilege whereby foreigners, established in Egypt and grown wealthy in Egypt, were exempt from taxes, should be abolished. The heartless fellow did not want those special courts of law for foreigners that, under the name of *mixed courts*, handed out two types of justice —honey for the European and gall for the Arab. This pernicious man in fact suggested that public positions should not be given exclusively to foreigners—and that over three thousand *contos* of good Egyptian money should not be paid, as it is at present, to Frenchmen and Englishmen and Italians installed in sinecures in all the government departments of the Nile Valley; most of these officials are as useful to the State as the Englishman who, with a letter of recommendation from Lord Palmerston, was appointed a colonel in the Egyptian Army and, at the end of nine years, after having received nearly eighty *contos* of salary, had still not seen his regiment *and did not even have a uniform*!

These then, in brief, were Arabi's wicked ideas, and it is not easy to imagine the full measure of indignation, of apoplexy they caused in republican France and freedom-loving England. Arabi was considered a monster. In the Exchanges of London and Paris, where Egyptian stock had declined, an immediate suppression of this iniquitous adventurer was called for.

The strident shouts of the foreigners in Egypt, their persons and privileges suddenly threatened, stirred all Europe to compassion.

The Western Powers 'exchanged views' as the hideous diplomatic phrase puts it, and agreed that Egypt was 'in a state of anarchy'. The Khedive had already declared himself 'under duress' and there was urgent need to come to the relief of this charming prince who was so beloved by foreign powers. So England and France (the countries which are said to have most interests in Egypt) sent their squadrons to the waters of Alexandria, to frighten Arabi. One might ask to what extent six battleships at anchor in a bay, without any troops to land, could frighten a Minister of War, secure in Cairo, ten hours away by railway, supported by four million Fellahin, allied to the great Bedouin leaders and sanctioned by the religious approval of the Ulema.

Today, those who advised mounting this show of force, like the *Times*, confess with a blush that it was ill-judged. At any rate it was done—with the support of a document, an absurd diplomatic note that could have come straight out of some farce by Labiche, so incredibly comic was its content. This Note, solemnly presented by the French and English, urged the Khedive to dismiss Arabi and exile him to Upper Egypt beyond the falls, allowing him in order not to deprive him of everything, to keep his title of Pasha and his colonel's salary! My friends, is not this the sort of lunacy you would find in a vaudeville act? On the one side you have the Khedive, abandoned in his palace, the victim of a victorious revolution, relying upon the somewhat doubtful protection of a few aides-de-camp and eunuchs; on the other side, Arabi supported by the army, the nation, the desert and the mosques. And Europe suggests that the Khedive should exile Arabi to Nubia! Can you imagine anything more fitting to the spirit of the much-lamented Offenbach? Today the English newspapers confess *sotto voce* that the Note was a mistake. It was indeed! And what was the result! Arabi shrugged his shoulders, arrogated for himself the post of Minister of the Navy, and in place of some of the other ministers, old friends of the Khedive, he substituted his own men of mettle and verve.

Well, this reply to their ultimatum took Europe down a

peg or two, if I may use such an irreverent expression. So then they took the decision made at moments of great crisis: they delegated diplomats to sit round a green-covered table with their heads thoughtfully in their hands. This was called the Conference of Constantinople. Its aim was praiseworthy: it was to solve the problem of Egypt.

And there it still sits, subtly, shrewdly, finding a solution! Alexandria has gone up in flames, ceased to exist; the Suez Canal is patrolled by English gunboats; General Sir Garnet Wolseley is marching on Cairo; Egyptian soil is now British soil—and there the Conference still sits, finding a solution! What skill it shows! What authority! There it still sits . . .

There it sits, on the banks of the waters of the Bosphorus, around a green-covered table, and its delegates rest their heads in their hands!

After the Conference was assembled Europe naturally remembered that Egypt is still a dependency of the Sultan's, and pays a tribute to the Sultan, whose duty it is to re-establish order when there are disturbances in his dominions.

This question of the relation between Egypt and Turkey is deep and complicated.

Is the Khedive a vassal prince? Diplomacy hesitates to decide. On the one hand the Khedives succeed one another by right of inheritance, they have an army and a navy, they coin money, they declare war and make treaties; on the other hand they pay a tribute. But does this argue a state of vassalage, as of a Pasha to his Sultan? Is the tribute a simple gift from a Moslem prince to the leader of Islam, like the present the Catholic King of

Spain sends every year to the Pope? Is it an annual instalment of an enormous sum, because Mohammed-Ali and later Ismail Pasha bought their independence from the Osmanli? Is it merely a gratuity? . . . Whatever it is, the tribute exists—and based upon this, Europe appealed to the Sultan. Arabi, good believer that he is, must venerate the Sultan; the Sultan, good father that he is, could exterminate Arabi. And here begins the famous comedy of the Sultan's vacillations.

The Sultan would, on the one hand, like to send troops to Egypt, occupy it on the pretext of restoring order, and then make it a Turkish province, a Pashalik dependent on the Seraglio, as it was before Mohammed-Ali, when the real treasure-house of the Caliphs lay in the valley of the Nile. On the other hand the Sultan would not wish to disembark in Egypt, like a policeman acting on behalf of Europe, because the Ulema, from the mosque of El-Azhar, the great religious centre and centre of the Arts in Islam—the Vatican and the Sorbonne of the East, which possesses in the Moslem world an authority equal to a Council in the Catholic world—had foreseen such an incident and declared that if the Sultan, in the name of Christian Europe, should take up arms against the Mohammedan people, he would, *ipso facto*, be regarded an apostate, and *ipso facto* he would lose the Caliphate. Furthermore the Sultan had, according to rumour, received promises from Arabi to depose the Khedive and proclaim in his place Helim Pasha, who is the counsellor and favourite of the Seraglio in Constantinople; so the Sultan conspired with Arabi against the Khedive. But on the other hand he had information that there was some understanding between Arabi and the Grand Shereef of Mecca, who, being a direct descendant of Mohammed, has more right to the Caliphate than the Sultan, and, in this holy claim he is supported by all the tribes in Arabia; fearing that Arabi might therefore become the cause of a schism in Islam, the Sultan sought to undermine his growing influence—and he conspired with the Khedive against Arabi. Yet again, any revolution in a Moslem country was held in horror by the Sultan; but on the other hand, the contemptuous way in which Arabi, the spirit behind this movement, was treating part of allied Europe deeply flattered his Turkish heart. Indeed, this unfortunate leader of the Faithful did not know where to turn his imperial head ... It must not be thought from my light manner of speaking that I do not respect the Sultan: Abdul-Hamid is not one of the old-style Caliphs, besotted by the enjoyment of three thousand women, but, according to Prince Bismarck, 'one of the sharpest minds in Europe'. Now Prince Bismarck is a connoisseur. In my view, however, two things spoil this famous sharpness he mentions: first, it goes too far, so that on most occasions Abdul-Hamid stumbles and falls victim to the ingenious, complicated plots he himself devises; second, he serves not practical ideas but mystical phantasies, like that which is attributed to him of renewing, both for religious reasons and for his own advantage, the prophetic empire of Mohammed.

So, pressed by Europe to intervene in Egypt, and not wanting to intervene because this would mean the loss of that profitable annual tribute, the Sultan decided to send Dervish Pasha, a scheming old fox, on a mission to bring

Arabi back to the fold. But scarcely had Dervish Pasha begun this operation than the Sultan, troubled by the vision of Arabi and the Grand Shereef of Mecca clasping hands over the Prophet's tomb, offered Arabi the Grand Order of Medjidie, the noblest Turkish decoration, the highest favour that the Caliph can bestow, and the honour was accompanied by a flowery letter of friendship and a splendid diamond.

This gives some idea of the Grand Turk's confusion.

Thus honoured by the Caliph, Arabi shone in the eyes of the Moslem world with even greater prestige; Dervish Pasha, momentarily put off his stroke, redoubled his duplicity; and then there was set in train, between Dervish and Arabi and the Khedive and the Sultan and the Powers and the consuls and the pashas and the colonels, such a tangled mesh of plotting that I should prefer to make a lucid summary of the twenty-five volumes of *Rocambole's Exploits* than try to penetrate the depths of this Turkish-European imbroglio: it is one of those wearisome intrigues which must get on the nerves of Divine Providence and make Him weep from sheer tedium if He, as certain philosophers who are on intimate terms with Him insist, is obliged to observe in minute detail all of human happenings! How man must, through his stupidity, make God yawn!

Throughout these events, while Europe wallowed in the diplomatic mire, the two squadrons, the French and the English, remained there off Alexandria, 'manifesting their presence'. From daybreak until sunset, motionless on the still waters, while the sailors' shirts dried on the yards, there they remained ...

The officers had an occasional rest from their stiff role as watchdogs, and arranged a picnic on land, or went for a rubber of whist at the English Club, or organized in the shade of the Ramleh gardens an honest game of cricket.

3

ORIENTAL EPISODE—MOSLEMS AND CHRISTIANS— A SOCIAL DUNG-HEAP—OPINIONS FROM ROUND THE TABLE—THE EUROPEAN CIVIL-SERVANTS IN CAIRO—ISMAIL PASHA'S DEBTS—JUNE 11TH

This was the state of affairs when June 11th dawned, which from henceforth in history—this brief instant of human notoriety which is emphatically called *history*—will be known as 'the massacre of Alexandria'.

The first Oriental incident I saw, when I disembarked in Alexandria twelve years ago, was at the Customs Quay, brilliant under the glare of the sun: a European employee, ostensibly European by his general appearance, by the coat he wore, and especially by the braided cap—was slashing the skin off an Arab's back with one of those hippopotamus-hide whips, known there as a *courbache* which, in Egypt, is the official symbol of authority.

Round about, as if this scene were not unusual or scandalous, other Arabs carried loads; other braided employees, whips in hand, gave their orders amidst cigarette smoke.

Bored or tired perhaps, the man with the *courbache*, who was a skinny fellow, directed a final kick at the Arab's posterior—as a person might add a full-stop to a sentence penned with particular verve—and turning towards my companion and myself, offered his respectful services, cap in hand. He was Italian and a charming fellow. Meanwhile the Arab, (like most of the Fellahin a superb figure of a man of sculptural form), after shaking himself as a Labrador shakes itself on leaving the water, went to crouch in a corner, his eyes shining like two coals, but nonetheless quiet and fatalistic in demeanour, surely thinking that Allah is great in heaven and the *courbache* and the foreigner are necessary on earth.

When I read those panicking telegrams of June 11th which announced to all Europe that the Arab population was massacring the Europeans in the streets of Alexandria —I do not know why I immediately saw again the Customs Quay and the Italian employee with the braided cap, and the *courbache* cracking on the Arab's dark shoulders. I do not intend this as an allegory, implying that the relations between Europeans and Egyptians is reduced to these two attitudes—an arm issuing from a fine white sleeve and wielding a *courbache*, and a half-naked back anticipating punishment: still less do I wish to insinuate that the 11th was the belated revenge for these bureaucratic brutalities . . .

Egypt is not Sierra Leone: and the Crescent has not yet been brought so low that it consents to being systematically beaten by the Cross. But the truth is that in Egypt any European employee in the Customs or at the docks, or on the railway, who would not dare to raise his hand against a European porter, will whip the skin off an Egyptian as naturally and with the same indifference as one would brush off a persistent fly.

The Alexandrian European considered the Egyptian Fellah a being of the lowest order, incapable of being civilized, a mere beast of burden; and if he had La Bruyère's style, he would have described him as La Bruyère described the peasants at the time of Louis XIV, 'dim shapes bent over the earth and having the vague semblance of human beings . . .'

When a man scorns his fellow like this, the *courbache* is used readily and insolence is the prevalent attitude.

And we must remember that the European had very little more respect for the Egyptian of the upper or cultured classes. The lowest-grade clerk at the Consulate would consider it beneath his dignity to give precedence to the oldest and noblest Sheik, leader of ten tribes and descendant of the Prophet; and the most insignificant employee in the Telegraph Office, a *Figaro* reader, would have nothing but disdain for the most learned doctors of the University of El-Azhar who do not go along to the café to read the *Figaro* and know little about telegraphy.

But this absurd disdain for a noble race, to whom civilization owes so much, is not found only among the Europeans in Alexandria, a colony of people washed ashore here from the various lands of the Mediterranean; did we not hear M. Gambetta declare only a few days ago, from the vantage point of the French government benches, that Sinai of the bourgeoisie, that the Egyptian people could only be governed by the whip?

The complicated wealth of our material civilization, our machines, our telephones, our electric light, have made us become intolerable pedants: we are ready to declare that a race is despicable if it does not know how to make Erard pianos; and if there is somewhere a people who have not, as we have, the talent for composing comic operas, we consider it *ipso facto* destined for perpetual slavery.

On the other hand, the Egyptians consider the Europeans as they did the last and most terrible plague of Egypt—another invasion of locusts descending upon them, not from the heavens, where the wrath of Jehovah rumbles, but from the steamships of the Mediterranean —spreading out and devouring the wealth of the Nile. And this prejudice is not peculiar to the uneducated classes: the most cultured of Pashas, educated in France, reading along with us the *Revue des Deux Mondes*, will refuse to recognize what Egypt owes to European energy and science and capital; for him, as for the meanest mule-driver in the Cairo markets, the European is more than an intruder—he is a thieving one.

The Arab does in no manner consider himself inferior to us: he is not dazzled by our industries and our inventions; and I am sure that from the calm repose of his harem, the great noise that we make upon the earth seems to him no more than a futile commotion. He feels for us the same amazement mingled with disdain that a philosopher might feel when he watches a juggler at work. The thinker acknowledges that he is incapable of balancing a rifle on his nose and he is sorry; but he consoles himself with the reflection that neither is the juggler able to put two ideas together. Similarly the Moslem must admire our gas and our gadgets, our barrel organs and all our mechanical skill; then he strokes his beard, smiles and thinks to himself: 'All that proves their patience and skill, but I have something better here within me, something greater even than the steam-power and electricity—the moral perfection that Mohammed's Law has given me.'

Moreover we know, from the romances we read in our youth, that the Crescent has always detested the Cross; and one can imagine the Moslem's feelings now that the Cross, instead of fighting them with the Paladins, exploits them with the money-lenders.

If the inoffensive tourist who wanders along with his purse at the ready, in cities like Damascus and Beirut, excites hostile stares and remarks, merely because everything in him is different, from the dogmas of his religion to the shape of his hat—one can imagine what happens in towns like Alexandria and Tunis, where the European is not a gentle tourist handing out tips, but a greedy negotiator who comes to settle there like a conqueror and make a small fortune for himself in no time, under the flag of his Consulate.

I should add that in Egypt the European appears in the eyes of the Arab as hatefully privileged.

One thing seemed particularly intolerable—that the European should get every job, every one of them, from fat sinecures down to modest positions earning a hundred francs a month.

Whenever any humble vacancy arose, like a postman or telegraphist, and an honest, hard-working Arab applied along with a scoundrel of Greek or Maltese nationality, who was the job given to? To the scoundrel, of course.

This system, productive at the beginning, when Egypt was a barbaric province of Turkey, and the Europeans were men of special learning and integrity, began in the time of Mohammed-Ali, who attempted to build a nation upon the ruins of the old Pashalik, inviting European science and capital to achieve his goal. It continued under Said Pasha, that delightful *bon-vivant*, such a Francophile that he spent his days concocting French puns and would not allow anyone in his presence or in the government offices, who was not gentleman enough to appreciate a *Charivari*; but the great invasion of European employees reached its peak at the time of Ismail Pasha—who accepted anything that came from Europe, the specialists and the beggars, those who brought an idea and those who brought only debts.

Egypt then re-enacted the old legend of El-Dorado. Anyone who found himself hounded by creditors, whether in Paris or London or Rome, when his last over-coat was going threadbare at the elbows, and he was no longer able to go back to his club because he owed the doorman ten francs, would get hold of some diplomat or prince to give him a letter of recommendation to the Khedive, and take the boat to Alexandria.

There he had his hotel paid by His Highness for the first few days—and at the end of the month a situation was found for him by His Highness. Anything: if he was an old drawing-room tenor, with no voice left, then he was appointed a colonel in the Cavalry; if he was a dis-credited soldier, he became a school inspector. The man who could not manage to obtain a letter for the Khedive would fling himself at the Consul's feet. If he dared not present himself to the Consul, he used the oblique influences of the Court—the most powerful ones—the eunuchs, the cooks, the dancing-girls . . . The job came, simple and lucrative. And the Fellah paid for the lot.

But worst of all were the higher civil-servants, those whom the Powers installed inside the Egyptian administration: so jealous were they of one another that if, for example, France managed to get a Frenchman into the Treasury, then England, to counterbalance this measure of influence, would push an Englishman into Naval Headquarters; and in her turn Italy, already suspicious, would wangle a son of Rome into the Department of Education. Some of these gentlemen naturally had some specialist training, but their great number clogged the movement of the administrative machine. It has been proved that the Khedive, yielding to these pressures, was obliged to have *six employees to do the simple work of one*! This little world in itself formed a state within the state.

In the Treasury, in the law-courts, in the military headquarters, in the commissions, in every nook and cranny of its administration, Egypt saw only foreign faces, heard only foreign tongues, was aware only of foreign interests; and it was Egyptian money which maintained all these people, who were there only to nullify Egyptian influence. And were these people at least useful? . . . The Consul General of the United States has told, in a recently-published book on Egypt, that he once dined in Cairo with six high officials, all of them foreigners, and whose total annual salaries amounted to nearly *one hundred contos*! In their departments, correspondence, book-keeping, everything was all done in the Arab language: *and not one of these men knew Arabic*!

*

There was perhaps no worse population in all the world

128

than that of Alexandria. This city, which in former days was the store-house of Oriental luxury and learning, had become in our days, under the Khedive Ismail Pasha, the refuse dump of southern Europe. All the human rubbish from Greece, the Islands of the Archipelago, Italy, Sicily and Marseilles (and Heaven knows what an abundance of scoundrels there is in these sites of classical beauty)—all this rubbish discharged itself instinctively onto Alexandria, to spread out and become under its beautiful deep blue sky a stinking social dung-heap.

One needed only to cross a street to appreciate how customs differed.

At each corner, a music-hall was packed with a filthy crowd shouting and smoking and tossing back brandy, while on the stage, above the foot-lights, a heavily-powdered matron with exposed bosom screeched out an obscene ditty ... One out of every ten houses was a brothel, screened from the street by a simple curtain ... Everywhere there was gambling: a trickster carried a little roulette and a chair and set up his game in the middle of the street; others immediately thronged around and in a few moments the police had to step in because blood began to flow ...

The educated, more discerning tourist had to hasten away from such an atmosphere and seek refuge in a quiet Moslem café, beside the calm water. There at least there were only Arabs gravely smoking their *chibouk* and talking together politely, behaving in general with dignity.

I remember the first table in Alexandria at which I ever sat talking. It was dominated by a Greek of pale countenance and side-whiskers shining like patent leather; a gold chain hung round his open collar and he sported brilliants, perhaps real ones, on the front of a shirt which he must have worn for a week! What a rogue he was! What a bandit! How that fellow must have dabbled in all the shady transactions and savoured all the orgies along the Levantine coast! And the best of it was, he talked of Egypt as a conquered country, a group of islands that were obliged to provide him with clothes and shoes and money to fill his pockets, his and the pockets of all those applauding him around the table, Europeans every one of them, middle-men, minor employees, plain beggars, all of them with gold watch-chains, open collars, their fat faces shining with evil, their voices full of swagger, petty Don Juans every one of them.

'*L'arabe, monsieur,*' said this equivocal gentleman to me, speaking French with a strong Piraeus accent, '*ce n'est qu'une infecte canaille!*'

You were the *infecte canaille*, you waxen Greek!

Surely what made Arabi most popular in Egypt was his hostility towards foreigners. *Egypt for the Egyptians!* That phrase, a whole programme, went to the very hearts of the whole race. Egypt for the Egyptians—not for the foreign employees, nor for the foreign money-lenders.

Ah! This question of creditors! The famous question of the Egyptian debt! How did Ismail Pasha spend those hundreds of millions which Europe lent him, and which the poor Fellah is still paying back? In the first place, it was in trying to put into practice an economic idea—the conversion of Egypt, which is an agricultural country, into an industrial nation. Egypt produced sugar—why not refine it? She had cotton—why not weave it? And he began, spending millions in the process, to cover the banks of the Nile with those colossal factories of which only ruins remain today—ruins of rusty iron and rotten wood, so miserable and so sad beside those magnificent granite ruins of the Pharaonic temples, and representing as the latter do, the servitude of a race, but unlike the latter, so ugly that they cannot serve now even for the subject of a water-colour.

The other cause of the Khedive's ruin was his extravagance, his legendary extravagance—who has not heard tell of it? Who does not remember the Suez Canal parties? Every budget was counted in millions! Two millions for the illumination of Cairo. Four millions for the Ismailia banquet. Expenses incurred with the two thousand guests for a fortnight in Cairo and on the Canal —seventy millions! For the champagne drunk during those weeks of revelry—two millions! And the Fellah paid.

Ah! And here I am talking, and I too drank that champagne that was in reality the sweat of the Fellah, sparkling and sweetened. I too was a guest of Ismail Pasha, at the Fellah's expense! I too ... Let us be silent, let us cover our foreheads with ashes and implore the Fellah's pardon!

*

The result of these industrial phantasies and the luxuries fit for Solomon was that Egypt found herself indebted to Europe by hundreds of millions, on which she paid an interest of seven per cent, and like the prudent bourgeois who zealously watches over his interests, Europe had gradually taken over the administration of Egypt.

When Arabi wanted to alter this system, which was changing the Egyptian people into a horde of slaves working for the financiers of Paris and London, squadrons from France and England appeared at once, demanding Arabi's exile, and the disbanding of the army, which was the instrument and strength of the national party. The Arabs saw in this a wicked abuse of strength, with England and France wishing to maintain by force the interests of those who held Egyptian bonds and the privileges of the intruders.

From that moment Arabi became the liberator; and the Khedive, whom the squadrons had come to protect against Arabi, became the renegade, the traitor.

That was the position on June 11th. Alexandria became a hot-bed. In the mosques they rabidly preached a crusade against the Christians: in the bazaars the foreigner was spoken of as a cursed dog, a bird of prey, worse than the locusts that devour the harvest in the fertile fields of the Nile; and either it was the fanaticism which was stirred up, or the misery which cried out for revenge—but every good Moslem took up arms.

Under circumstances like these a civil war could be born from a jest in a coffee-house. And that is more or less what happened. On the morning of the 11th, in Rue des Soeurs, one of the richest streets in the European district, an Englishman, from force of habit, whipped an Arab, but against all tradition, the Arab responded by clubbing him. The Englishman fired his revolver. In a few moments the conflict between Europeans and Arabs had exploded in all its fury and spread over the entire district. This lasted five hours—until the army, which had remained neutral until then, received telegraphed orders from Cairo and settled the disturbance. And the result, unexpected but understandable, since the Arabs were known to have only clubs and the Europeans rifles, was this: nearly a hundred Europeans were killed, but over three hundred Arabs were slaughtered. The newspapers have called this *The Massacre of the Christians*: I have no wish at all to appear churlish to my brothers in Christ, but I must point out that this should rather be called the *Slaughter of the Moslems*.

4

THE FLIGHT OF THE EUROPEANS—THE GREAT
ENGLISH DREAM—THE 'CASUS BELLI'—
THE EVE OF THE BOMBARDMENT

This massacre of the Christians—to continue with the diplomatic nickname—swiftly drew every newspaper-reader's attention towards Egypt; all the incidents that in one week of chaos and high drama crowded one upon the other must still be so living and present to the memory that it is unnecessary to repeat all the details. There was the loud and excessive indignation of Europe, excited by the clamour of the English press; the uncontrollable panic which took hold of the European residents in Egypt; and, what is strange even in this land from where the great Exodus took place, the way in which a colony of over one hundred thousand souls suddenly forsook the soil where they had been settled for generations, leaving behind occupations, interests, employment, home and estate, and rushed terrified to the docks to crowd into steamships and cargo-boats and barges—whatever vessel, regardless of shape or size, that could float on the water— and escape from that unlucky land, paying their weight in gold for the right to huddle in a corner of the hold. Then there was the imperious way England, through its naval officers, organized and controlled this modern flight of the Hebrews; finally, the arrival in Alexandria of the Khedive, who had lost all his authority in Cairo and taken the opportunity of bringing the tattered remains of his royal dignity to shelter under the cannons of Admiral Seymour.

Arabi Pasha, who had in fact become a dictator, also made his hasty way to Alexandria—and his first step was to set up Courts Martial to try those guilty of the massacre of the 11th.

It should be noted that this was not, by any means, a matter of punishing the Europeans who had sent three hundred Moslems from this land of sorrows to Allah's Paradise: but of dealing only with those Moslems who were suspected of having laid violent hands upon Christians. Even so, the English newspapers cried out straightway that they could have no confidence in the justice of this trial, in the impartiality of the Egyptian magistrates, as hostile to the foreigner as to the Egyptian populace, and that these judgements were no more than a farce: those found guilty would be laden with make-believe chains and displayed to European eyes, and afterwards, behind the scenes, would be acclaimed as loyal patriots.

Arabi Pasha then proposed that these courts be made up of Arab judges and English officers. This showed a strong desire, a greed I could almost say, for justice. And indeed, if the National Party, all-powerful as it was then, did not prove how strict it was, it would risk incurring the accusation of being an accomplice; and if its reforms had already been greeted unfavourably by Europe, what would happen if such crimes could plausibly be attributed to it?

Moreover, for a noble, orthodox Moslem like Arabi, any form of violence against a foreigner, against a guest, would constitute the gravest violation of Holy Law. Arabi was sincere. But England did not accept his proposals.

England did not accept. England was armed on board its battleships. And yet, more than any other nation, she had suffered from the tumults of Alexandria: the British Consul, brutally beaten, was said to be dying; some of the ships' officers had received on their uniform, which is the pride of Great Britain, mud and stones flung by the hands of the Egyptian people; the majority of the Europeans killed were of British nationality; and war was being urged against England in the mosques, in the bazaars, and even under the Bedouin's tent.

But England, generous and paternal as she was, wished to forget these insults. And with very good reason!

The fact is that it did not suit her convenience to recognize the atrocities of the 11th as merely a casual outbreak of Moslem fanaticism, which a hanging or two and some chains could put an end to; nor did it suit her convenience to disembark from her battleships merely to go to a court of law to help sentence a dozen or so criminals.

What did suit England's convenience was to magnify this local disturbance to the proportions of a general state of national anarchy, and to offer, or impose, her aid not to punish a few local criminals but to pacify a whole country

135

which was in a state of turmoil. So she jubilantly greeted this long-desired day, so patiently awaited since the beginning of the century, so anxiously hoped for since the opening of the Suez Canal—the day when she would finally be given a pretext to place her iron-shod foot on Egyptian soil, to place on it her great Anglo-Saxon paw which, once put on foreign soil—whether it be a rock like Gibraltar, or a stretch of sand like Aden, or an island like Malta, or a whole world like India—no human effort could ever again hope to budge.

This was no longer a matter of liberating the Khedive, of protecting the pockets of Egypt's creditors. A higher interest, connected with the destinies of the Empire, was awoken and dominated everything.

Egypt was in a state of anarchy: it was the duty of England, Paladin of civilization, to restore order and prevent it from falling again into its barbaric state.

Egypt was in a state of anarchy: it was the duty of England, as a great Eastern power, to defend this precious area of Egyptian territory, the Suez Canal, and prevent its falling into the hands of Arabi of some other Moslem dictator hostile to the benefits of civilization.

This is more or less what England replied, and in a loud voice so that all the world should hear, when Arabi Pasha proposed a judicial alliance to punish the Moslem crime of the 11th.

'No,' said John Bull, 'this has nothing to do with the 11th! Let us forget the 11th. Let us forget it, as if it were merely the 7th. The question is this: *Egypt is in a state of anarchy*. Civilization must be protected!'

And, stripped of their humanitarian adornments, these

noble words meant that England, under this pretext of pacifying Egypt, would disembark in Alexandria and occupy for military purposes Port-Said and Suez—the Canal's two ports; and then, never again would the English flag be struck from those two vital steps on the route to India!

And that would mean the fulfilment of Britain's great dream: absolute possession of the route to India; John Bull on guard duty at all the successive gateways that lead to her Empire in the East: at the entrance to the Mediterranean, Gibraltar and her invincible rock; in the Mediterranean, Malta and Cyprus, two islands, two colossal war depots: at the entrance to the Canal, Port-Said; at the end of the Canal and at the mouth of the Red Sea, Suez; at the edge of the Persian Gulf, Aden; and from there onwards her squadrons sweeping the seas.

And after the carnage of Alexandria, England did indeed find this splendid opportunity before her; and having at once officially declared Egypt in a state of anarchy, she began, without losing a moment, to arm herself.

And in the midst of all this, what about Europe? Oh! England invited Europe with fine disinterested gestures, to share with her the honour of pacifying Egypt! But she was well aware that not one of the Great Powers would send one soldier to help: not even France, who had a fleet in the bay of Alexandria and had collaborated in those Platonic demonstrations; France, governed by a bourgeois democracy which had grown rich and become one vast business concern, did not want, at any cost, to disturb that sweet calm peace in which her millions were ripening.

Apart from this, the powers had already salved their

dignity as, seated around the green conference table beside the luminous waters of the Bosphorus, they meditated, head in hands, on possible solutions to the Egyptian question. As for the rest, they were watching, armed to the teeth, suspicious and jealous, hating each other but reciprocally immobilized by the very magnitude of the armaments.

France fears Germany; Turkey fears Russia; Austria is hemmed in between the two; Italy needs everyone's goodwill; and everyone in their turn trembles before Bismarck, the dreadful bogey-man, the Jupiter thundering from the diplomatic Olympus, who in his retreat in Varzin, plagued by all sorts of illnesses, spends part of his time under the influence of morphine.

That they all fancied Egypt's spoils no one can doubt unless he ignore the instinct to rob, pillage and cheat which nests in the soul of every civilized race; but none of the other Powers is, like England, an island surrounded by a rough sea, the domain of the world's greatest fleet; and, confined as they were in a small continent, shoulder to shoulder and sword against sword, none of them dared to venture a step in Egypt's defence, for fear that his neighbour might leap at his throat. They were therefore reduced to exchanging phrases of diplomatic courtesy as they sat, full of rancour, around their conference table.

When those who fancy the riches contained in a locked-up house stand outside, pen in hand, discussing the best way of getting in, the prize goes to the one who arms himself with a hatchet instead of a pen and aims the first blow at the door. That is what England did. While the others drew up theoretical plans she opened fire on Alexandria.

The only thing is, one cannot attack an inoffensive city without a pretext. And England was forced to give such a bad one, lacking a better, that, as the Association of English Positivists said in their protest against the invasion of Egypt, her puerility managed only to enhance her immorality.

If Arabi Pasha did not understand England's predatory intentions, he must at least have concluded that the preparations she was making were against him, against the party he was leading, and against the ideas he embodied; and very naturally, expecting an attack, he organized a defence, furnishing Alexandria's forts with artillery and setting up new batteries along the coast.

And it was against this that England protested; it was out of this that she made her *casus belli*, declaring that unless the works on the forts ceased, she would destroy the forts! Although not at war with Egypt, she considered she had the right to assemble a threatening fleet in front of Alexandria; but she would not allow the authorities of Alexandria even to repair the breaches in the old fortifications erected by Mohammed-Ali!

And what fantastic explanations Mr Gladstone gave Europe, to justify her *casus belli!* The batteries that Arabi was setting up, he said, the new cannons he was positioning, *were putting the English battleships in peril!* And were the battleships not endangering the forts? But beside the English squadron there were French, German, Italian, Greek and Austrian warships—as exposed to Arabi's cannons as those that hoisted the British flag: and these did not consider themselves 'in peril'!

What would England say if the captain of one of those French or German battleships, which from time to time are anchored in the waters of Portsmouth or Southampton, suddenly forbade the governor of one of these fortified places to continue the defence-works which they are incessantly perfecting, on the pretext that these batteries could damage the ship under his command? ... With such a precedent English admirals, who frequently honour the humble port of Lisbon by the presence of their flags, would be authorized to demand the destruction of the Towers of St Julian and Bugio and Belém! One might say that it is unlikely that the Portuguese, peaceful and good-natured fellow that he is, would fire his cannons—least of all upon English battleships. I agree. But what would Arabi Pasha gain by shooting a few surprise cannon-balls at the English squadron—and therefore at the others which were anchored in the same place—unless it were to call upon himself and his party and his country the fearful vengeance of all Europe, every flag of which would feel outraged.

Arabi did a wise thing: he yielded, and promised to interrupt the defence-works. And England was disappointed. Arabi's submission upset their ingenious plan.

Some newspapers, the most cynical and impatient ones, went so far as to advise their government not to take the word of a vile Moslem—and *to start the bombardment*! So the task of the fleet was now to keep a sharp and incessant watch upon the fortifications, in the hope of discovering some sapper, spade raised, to prove that Arabi was breaking his word. At night the battleships shone long bright rays of electric light upon the coast, moving them slowly over the batteries, delving anxiously into the smallest corners, searching for the slightest sign of work—even if it were no more than an abandoned hamper of stones; and thus it was that one night—a happy night for Mr Gladstone's government!—the squadron discovered two soldiers cleaning an old cannon! What a relief for England! Immediately Admiral Seymour sent this ultimatum to Toulba Pasha, governor of the city: within twenty-four hours the forts were to be handed over to British troops, or the whole line of battleships would open fire upon Alexandria. And really the only answer to this is the one given by Cambronne at Waterloo.

I am sorry that Arabi did not say it: it would have been the second time in history that John Bull received it full in the face.

The eve of the bombardment was a dramatic one. Admiral Seymour made all the merchant ships leave the bay; and then, with his usual courtesy, he invited the warships of other nations to move away, taking their neutral flags out of the line of fire. The long procession of battleships from all Europe, slowly leaving the waters of Alexandria so that England could commit her outrage in peace, is described by the English correspondents as a scene full of solemnity and ceremony. The salutes of the guns resounded one after the other; one by one the admirals' flags dipped to each other. The last to leave were the French ships, their allies in the 'demonstration', who, may it be to their credit, had no wish to be allies in this crime: and the tricolour also moved away, saluted by Admiral Seymour, amid the hurrahs! of the sailors' farewell and the blare of the *Marseillaise*. The afternoon was beautiful; the bay was filled with light; the minarets of Alexandria shone white against the blue . . . A magnificent spectacle without a doubt: but what were the thousands of poor Arabs there thinking, the women and children who gazed at it from the heights of the city, those Arabs upon whom the shells and cannon-balls were to fall the following day?

Finally night descended and the stars came out; at the edge of the calm water the lights of Alexandria shone; everything was silent in the bay.

They were alone, face to face, under the peace of the heavens, a large English squadron and the inoffensive city which, the following morning, to satisfy the greed of a nation of shop-keepers, it was going to raze to the ground in cold blood.

5

AFTER THE SHELLING—THE FIRES—THE
RESPONSIBILITIES—AN ENGLISH ALEXANDRIA—THE
INVASION—THE ATTITUDE OF EUROPE

Admiral Seymour had declared some days before that in two short hours he would demolish the forts of Alexandria. However, after nine long hours, he had still not silenced the Egyptian batteries; and a shell had even blasted open the captain's cabin in the *Inflexible*.

Sir Beauchamp Seymour recognized, in his despatches to the Admiralty, that 'the best artilleries in Europe could be proud of such a fine resistance.' But neither courage nor fortifications nor granite walls could prevail against those black monsters which disfigure the seas—the *Monarch*, the *Alexandra*, the *Superb*, the *Sultan*, the *Invincible*, the *Minotaur*, and the rest that were there—mobile castles of iron, served by the combined forces of steam, hydraulics and electricity, as devastating as a cataclysm and exact as a science.

Poor fortresses of Mohammed-Ali! It was like the old fable of the metal pot falling on top of the earthenware pot. When night fell, only silent heaps of smoking ruins remained.

The deed was done! A great peace lay over the bay now; night fell, calm and dark; the enormous battleships lay at rest; not the slightest noise came from the vanquished city! Only the palace of Ras-el-tin blazed helplessly from a hill-top. It was then that the eloquent correspondent of the *Standard* telegraphed to his newspaper these memorable words: 'The situation could not be more satisfactory!'

During the night, however, from the part of Alexandria where Consuls' Square was, a great light began to spread. A fire had evidently broken out there. But how? Why?

Admiral Seymour would wash his hands of this—if he had Pontius Pilate's wash-bowl on board. He had scrupulously concentrated his attack upon the forts: a shell or two might have fallen in the Arab quarters—what could be more legitimate, inflicting a little salutary terror! But the European part of Alexandria had been spared ... And yet it was there that the red glow was spreading, heating the sky; and from other points nearby giant flames were darting up into the night. What the devil! The situation was not so satisfactory after all ...

143

The next day was very cloudy and the sea was rough. The battleships took the precaution of moving further off. When, some hours later, they came back to take up their fighting position once more, Alexandria was flaring up in front of them like a monstrous bonfire. The situation was most certainly not at all satisfactory now!

By no means. Arabi Pasha had abandoned Alexandria, taking with him most of the army. And the Moslem population, maddened by nine hours of bombing, encouraged by the Ulema and without police to control them, rushed to the European quarter and set the place alight and sacked and killed and destroyed, for they were greedy now for pillage and inflamed by the fury of the reprisals; they killed for the sake of killing, for even poor cart-horses were found quartered; they destroyed for the sake of destroying, for women's dresses and clocks and opera-glasses were found in pieces in the streets.

These were acts of violence committed in a state of paroxysm which takes a wild indiscriminate vengeance upon everything that represents the race, the customs and the ideas that it hates—upon the men and upon whatever represents them. This does not happen only in a Moslem country. When the Parisians invaded the Tuileries they slashed the satin of the chairs with their swords.

Can we consider the population of Alexandria, then, because of these excesses, beyond the bounds of humanity? The English say so. I say that we should have done the same, we Europeans, Christian as we are and rotten with civilization. If, when the Germans were bombing Paris, the Parisians had seen an exclusively German quarter in the midst of their city, compact, monumental, luxurious, built with the money that the Germans had accumulated by exploiting France—would the Parisians, the most civilized of mortals, have resisted swamping it with paraffin and setting it alight one beautiful winter's night?

The answer is simple, if we remember that when M. Thiers, that insignificant little statesman, attacked Paris, the Parisians hastened to destroy M. Thiers' palace.

Was it on Arabi's orders that Alexandria was set on fire? Evidently not. Arabi is not the savage type of patriot, like Rostopchin who burnt Moscow: although a Fellah, he is intelligent and wise, and knows that in Europe, and in England especially, where we affect a humanitarian sensitivity, there is nothing which brings more discredit than an act of cold cruelty. One has only to observe the polite, almost paternal attitude which he adopts with English prisoners—Midshipman Chair, for example. When this officer was taken to the Arab encampment, Arabi told him as soon as they had shaken hands: 'Write to your mother, and tell her you are in safe hands, so that she does not worry ...'

This was certainly sincere, and clever too: for these words went straight to the heart of every English mother. After the fighting in Alexandria Arabi has endeavoured to protect all the Europeans who still remain in the inland villages. The Cadis who did not stop the massacre of the railway officials of the Delta were executed. It is due to him that Cairo is calm, where there is an enormous amount of European property and wealth. What would Arabi have gained by destroying this prosperous Egyptian city at the beginning of his campaign and with his army intact? Merely the reputation of an ignorant monster.

The responsibility of the catastrophe lies with England. Perhaps the Admiral's shells did not, indeed, destroy more than a few poor Arab houses; but the ruin of Alexandria was caused by his government's imprudence.

From mid-June onwards, the most experienced and trustworthy of their diplomats, Mr E. Malet, Consul-General of Egypt, kept saying that if the bombardment was inevitable, then Sir Beauchamp Seymour should have troops ready to disembark and occupy the city as soon as the forts were destroyed so as to prevent Alexandria's being left at the mercy of a half-savage mob, in the probable event of Arabi retreating into the interior.

Nothing was done about it.

Sir Beauchamp Seymour bombarded and wrecked Alexandria, and virtually expelled Arabi from it, Arabi and the only body of men who could have controlled a population of a hundred thousand fanatics; and then he stayed on board his battleship calmly watching one of the richest cities in the Mediterranean burn in front of him.

And who benefited from this fire? England. The pretext that the forts 'put the British battleships in peril', entitled her, in the eyes of Europe, only to destroy the forts, and not to occupy the city. Now, however, now that the city was in flames, abandoned to anarchy and plundering, and to attack by Bedouin hordes which sprang out of the desert—*now* she had the right, indeed the duty, to disembark and save so much wealth, so splendid a commercial centre from total annihilation!

Generous England! And she immediately disembarked, found quarters for her soldiers, hoisted her flag. She had a heap of ruins before her, and within a few days she was building a new Alexandria in a British style now and with a British administration.

The fires were brought under control; the streets were cleared of rubble; an awesome police force was set up, which summarily executed pillagers and incendiaries; the city was supplied with food; the Customs opened its doors once more; stalls were put up to replace shops which had been destroyed; the judicial machine was set in motion again, the gas-works were repaired and the city illuminated; banks were open to business again.

And as it was necessary to have someone in authority, in the name of whom the city should be reorganized, the English, who were merely there (so they said) as a police force, went to fetch the Khedive from a house in the suburbs where he had sought refuge during the bombardment, and solemnly installed him in the Ras-el-tin Palace, a place half-burnt down from which the Khedive exercised a half-dead authority!

From that moment the situation became clearly defined and very simple. The English had possession of, and governed, Alexandria, as naturally as if it were situated in Yorkshire; and opposite Alexandria, on that sort of sandy isthmus which connects it to the land of the Delta, Arabi's encampment was dug in, controlling from this position all the valley of the Nile and the desert as far as the sea. The English received incessant reinforcements from home and from India. Arabi called up all the Fellahin to war against the English. England prepared to mount an invasion. Arabi organized a great national defence. Nothing clearer. The question is between England, trying to establish a protectorate in Egypt and snatch its strategic cities which control the Canal, and Arabi Pasha, a patriot, who wants Egypt for the Egyptians, who fears the protection of the foreigner as the worst disgrace for a weak country, and who cannot believe that the fact of Alexandria, Port-Said and Suez unfortunately being on the route to India is a motive for their being turned into English garrisons. Plenty of enthusiasm from both sides.

In London, where the season had ended and the monotony of the bathing beaches was beginning, the setting sail to conquer Egypt came to be considered a fine adventure. If the War Office had allowed them, all the golden youth, or merely the gilt, would have enlisted, because it was thought very *chic* to go to fight Arabi!

The Duke of Connaught, one of the sons of Her Majesty, is going with the expedition, and the Duke of Teck, his brother-in-law, not being a military man, went as a simple postal-officer, so it is said. The officers of the Guards, this cream of the aristocracy, and finest offspring of financiers, had the joy of seeing their magnificent regiments sent to Egypt; their natural pleasure was only partly spoilt by the severity of the War Office which, as this was a campaign and not a tournament, would not allow these gentlemen to be accompanied by baggage, liveried man-servants, luxury tents and crates of champagne.

One of these officers expressed his indignation very forcibly because the General Staff allowed him only three saddle-horses, two personal servants and five trunks!

On the other side, all along the Nile, the whole Fellahin population came out in favour of Arabi, as did, moreover, the educated classes, the Mosques, the Ulema, the Copts, and even the princes of the Khedive's family. The Mudirs, governors of the provinces, are paying their taxes to him. The sheiks of the desert send him their cavalry.

And their ardour is the greater for Arabi Pasha has been long prophesied; his unexpected entrance into the government is considered a divine advent; and this rebel (as other rebels who so gloriously made their way on earth and in heaven) is claimed to be the Messiah!

An ancient Moslem prophecy claims that in the thirteenth century of Hegira, a man of low birth would be born beside a great river, and his name would be called Ahmet, and he would rebel and would restore the splendour of Islam; now the Arabs are in the thirteenth century of Hegira, and Arabi, whose real name is Ahmet, and whose origin is Fellahin, was born in a village on the banks of the Nile, and rebelled against his Caliph. So he combines the dual prestige of a Spartacus and a Christ.

With the question concentrated now between a powerful invading nation and a patriot defending his soil, Europe took her traditional attitude: that is, she murmured a few mild words of warning and then retreated afar to watch how a strong arm makes the best of her strength, and study how a weak one is stripped of its rightful possessions.

In the last fifteen years Prussia stole Denmark and then went through Germany sacking kingdoms and duchies; next it dismembered France; later Russia broke up Turkey; two years ago the French Republic suddenly fell upon Tunis, and seized this unfortunate Berber state. In each one of these cases Europe behaved like a chorus in a traditional opera, when the stout baritone, round about the fourth act, raises his sword against the handsome, slight tenor: the choir modulates a long phrase, waves its arms in time, makes a bitter comment on the action, and perhaps shouts 'Stop!' Then, moving very sedately away, they leave the bearded tyrant at the footlights, calmly sinking his sword into the gallant's breast . . .

*

Let us speak no more of Europe. There is no Europe, there never has been, in the sense that this word has in diplomacy. Today there is a great forest where steel-clad bandits wander, loathing each other, fearing each other and by some tacit agreement allowing each other to advance each in his turn—and fall upon some poor devil vegetating or working in the corner of his yard. Along the wide and well-constructed highways of International Law, illuminated by Ortolan and other bright lights, armed robberies are blatantly carried out and at every moment the shouts of murdered peoples can be heard. Europe should be covered with the warning signs written up boldly at English race-tracks: BEWARE OF PICK-POCKETS!

Political small-holdings are coming to an end. The whole of the earth will shortly be in the hands of four or five great land-owners. Yesterday it was Tunis—because France needed to protect the frontier of Algeria. Today it is Egypt, because England needs to secure the route to India. Tomorrow it will be Holland—because Germany cannot live without colonies. Then Serbia—for motives that Austria in her turn will give. Later still Roumania—because Russia is strong. Then Belgium—because that is the way things go. Then . . .

This is a gloomy subject. Let us get back to the valley of the Nile!

6

SITUATION OF THE ARMY—THE NILE, THE
DROUGHT, THE DESERT—THE DANGERS OF A
'JIHAD'—MOSLEM SCEPTICISM—THE WORLD
GROWS ENGLISH—JOHN BULL'S ARROGANCE

Face to face they stand
The two brave camps . . .

This melancholy little song which, if I remember rightly, bewails the tragedy of Alcácer-Quibir, serves to portray graphically the strategic position of the English and the Egyptians since the beginning of the campaign.

To understand the situation better, let us imagine a large A. The internal triangle of the letter is the Delta—the land loved by the gods and so rich that in former days it alone was sufficient to furnish food for the whole Roman Empire; at the top of the letter stands Cairo—so that a Persian poet could fancifully say that the Delta is a green fan held by a diamond clasp, which is called Cairo. At the bottom of the right leg of the A, Alexandria stands and there part of the English army waits, defended by the fortifications of Ramleh; and in front of it, a cannon-shot away, is the large entrenched camp of Arabi Pasha, called Kraf-Daonar, comprising eighteen thousand Egyptians and enormous artillery parks, which prevents any approach along the Delta. The other part of the English army, commanded by the Commander-in-chief himself, Sir Garnet Wolseley, made its way by sea to the base of the left leg of the A, which is more or less Ismailia, and from there moved up this line to Kassassine, where it halted and made a fortification. Yet another enormous camp is entrenched a short distance away at Tel-el-Kebir, where Arabi has fifteen thousand men. And these four camps, situated opposite each other, and watching each other, make up the war in Egypt today.

To reach Cairo, then, his military and political objective, Sir Garnet has to take the Egyptian-held Kraf-Daonar if he wishes to move up the Delta—and Tel-el-Kebir, if he wishes to advance by the desert.

So far the four camps have gone no farther than exchange a few random shots in a skirmish or two. The London newspapers naturally write up these sniping incidents between the front lines in bold headlines, complete with lithographed maps and purple prose—making more ado than if the Battle of Waterloo were being fought again; but this, of course, is done simply to increase sales.

The Egyptians, entrenched in their camps, can count upon powerful allies: from the side of the Delta they can trust in the Nile, the ancient and good-natured Nile, which cannot fail to be faithful to those whom it has nourished for centuries, and which in a very short while will flood the lands of the Delta and, aided by Arabi's engineers who will surely obstruct the canals, will convert this route to Cairo into an immense stretch of impassable mud; this route would be the most favourable for the

English, for it would mean marching through rich, endless farmlands, between orchards and gardens, shaded paths and full granaries. From the side of the desert the Egyptians can count upon the sun, upon the drought and the sand. One can imagine what these troops from the cold North will suffer, marching over burning stretches of sand, in blinding, stunning light, under so torrid a heat that the metal stirrups scorch the boots; and the only water to drink there is muddy water which has to be boiled first! Sun-stroke and dysentry and nostalgia are already decimating the regiments, and as the English Commissariat, never very good, has had difficulties with transport, the troops of Her Majesty Queen Victoria have already suffered hunger! Ah! The route to India costs dear!

Apart from these allies that he possesses in Nature, Arabi counts on the Bedouin tribes, and in those nomadic hordes of Arabs on horseback who are coming from Tripoli to fight 'the foreign dog'; they amount to a reinforcement, he says, of thirty thousand men.

The English, for their part, count only on themselves. And this is no mean consideration. As their famous warsong goes, 'they have the ships, they have the men, they have the money, too.' They also have those magnificent Indian troops who can scoff at the sun, at the drought and at the deserts of Africa. And this led Sir Garnet to declare that the campaign would be finished by September 15th. It is true that it is already September 7th and he, entrenched at Kassassine, with the formidable barrier of Tel-el-Kebir before him, is still begging for reinforcements. But this proves only that this confounded war, having different habits from Caesar's, 'came and saw and *re-flected*'. Let us give him another month; let us give him three at the most; what is certain is that by the end of the year Arabi, his fields and his army and his happy aspiration to an Egyptian nationality, all this will have disappeared—as a cloud disappears in that dry African sky.

The English might suffer set-backs and lose thousands of men and spend thousands of pounds; but once the honour of its flag is at stake, and the chance of increasing the Empire, they will not sheathe their sword until they have installed in the fortress of ancient Cairo, to the strains of *God Save the Queen*, an English governor.

Evidently Mr Gladstone talks merely of re-establishing order and restoring the Khedive. Mere diplomatic parlance. The *Times*, which is England's mouthpiece, speaks plainly of a *protectorate*. And there are many Englishmen, even less reserved than the *Times*, who speak frankly of a *conquest*.

Even if Mr Gladstone, who is, in his way, a democrat within the limits of the Gospels, and his worthy colleague Lord Granville, who is a lawyer and a diplomat, should wish, for the sake of liberalism, Europe, international law and other vague things, to let Egypt re-organize herself—leaving the country empty-handed after having put down Arabi and his turbulent party—the whole of England *en bloc* would protest against such philosophical disinterestedness.

Is there anyone so ingenuous as to suppose that John Bull, that tower of commonsense, would consent to having his army decimated and his money spent as if it were water while the income-tax was being increased—

simply so that the Khedive, that charming young man, should continue to smoke his hubble-bubble of power in the shady gardens of the Choubra? John Bull will not be satisfied with anything less than a solid, long-lasting result: an *English Egypt*, and, running through its territory, like a corridor in a private house, the Suez Canal, the route to India. A government which, after burying millions of English pounds and thousands of English lives in the sands of Africa, will not offer this, will instantly receive John Bull's boot in its posterior.

But suppose a defeated Arabi manages to persuade the Shereef of Mecca to proclaim a *Jihad* against England— that is, a holy war, a crusade, a rising *en masse* of the whole Mohammedan world?

Certain good souls in England consider this a great danger—for in India alone there are fifty million Mohammedans. I do not believe, however, that there is any reason for John Bull to quail here. And I am sorry for that! Because this idea of a *Jihad* is a most picturesque one, with all its ceremony—the Shereef of Mecca unfurling the green flag of Mohammed, all the doctors of Islam present at the fateful *Fetiva*, and then straightway, from all corners of Asia and Africa, the torrent of believers rushing forth in the name of Allah! Wonderful subject for an ode—but one which unfortunately has no reality behind it.

In the first place—it never happens! The Crescent has often been humiliated by the Cross, Islam has received many a slap in the face from Christian Europe, and the Caliph has repeatedly spoken of proclaiming a *Jihad*— and yet the Prophet's standard remains rolled up in the sanctuaries of Mecca. And it is my opinion that if it were unfurled one day—it would be merely one more piece of green cloth fluttering in the breeze.

And would you like to know why? Because I believe the Moslems are as sceptical at this moment as we are, we Christians. In the sands of the desert, as in our gas-lit squares, it is no longer easy to find a thousand men who will gladly take up arms in the name of their God.

It is true that every good Moslem, at certain hours of the day, turns toward Mecca and prostrates himself in the ritual manner: purely a question of education, of good manners, of habit, as we Christians take off our hats when passing a village crucifix. Or else it is a vague superstition, a vague nervous gesture, like certain philosophers and positivists of my acquaintance who always make the sign of the cross as they hop out of bed.

One can already see, with the *Koran*, the melancholy case of a divine law falling into disuse. The Sultan receives ambassadors to dinner and he drinks champagne with them; the Cairo police arrest the holy vagrant dervishes, and the fast of Ramadan is no longer respected.

As with our own Gospel, the word of Mohammed is becoming an object of poetry, of commentary, of controversy. There are Renans in Islam; and the divine word, once analysed, no longer inspires the faith which can lead to death.

The Moslem world is in its thirteenth century, in the fullness of its middle age in fact, and surely there is many a Bedouin in his tent as faithful and steeped in Mohammed as those simple souls who so little time ago in the silence of our cloisters, wept over the Passion of Jesus; but I do not believe that even these patriarchs would leave their oases, their flocks and harems to come of their own free will, with no other pay than the sweet smile of the *houris* from the Garden of Paradise, to meet the fire from Krupp's cannons. And as for the cultured classes of Constantinople and Cairo and Smyrna and Tunis—these believe in the promise of the *houris* about as much as we in Regent Street believe in the green palms of heavenly bliss and in the Heavenly Choir.

Throughout the world religion is ebbing out from our souls; and all that remains is a vague religious feeling, created in part by the way our hearts have been disturbed by so long a subjection to the supernatural, and in part by the confused terror which reigns in this great universe which surrounds us, which is so simple and yet so little understood. In such a negative state, one of passivity in the face of doubt, an impulse to strong action is not easily awakened. A *Jihad* in Islam is as impracticable as a Crusade in the Christian world. Peter the Hermit would have finished up these days in a reformatory for having disturbed the public peace and international relations; and the fanatics who even today stand at the doors of the mosques in Cairo, yelling insults, urged on by their doctrine, against the foreign tourist, are immediately hauled off to gaol *for making a public disturbance*!

Mohammed in their mosques and Christ in our chapels, are growing singularly old; our Messiahs are gradually getting covered with the dust lifted by the strong breeze of reason, fashioning a new world; and the prophet of Islam, having lost the strength of his unity,

157

subdivided into a thousand minor prophets which preside over a thousand different sects, has difficulty in resisting the slow advance of western civilization. And with Christ and Mohammed, who constituted the active, vital forces in their religion, the vital and the militant is disappearing from our religions. God remains, Allah remains. Sublime abstractions but incapable of inspiring love or heroism.

What most makes divinity beloved is the amount of humanity which surrounds it. Clovis fought for Jesus, who had a breast like his, and in this human breast five open wounds; Suleiman would die happily for Mohammed, who was a warrior like him, and like him loved beauty.

But who is going to fight for God or Allah, these entities so vast that they fill all the heavens and so minute that they are not sufficient to satisfy our hearts, and which are subordinate to us, because they are made in our image, and are extended with all their weaknesses to the infinite in the depths of our souls?

Perhaps I am attributing to stout hearts of Mecca and the desert the literate scepticism of Pall Mall and the Boulevard de la Madeleine. What do we know of what goes on inside Islam? As little as the learned men of the mosque of El-Azhar know of what goes on here within our own confused Catholicism.

*

But even if a *Jihad* were organized it would only mean England spending a few more millions and sacrificing a few more regiments. Not the Koran, nor the famous green banner, nor Mohammed himself if he returned to earth to unfurl it, would prevent John Bull settling himself in Egypt now.

He is there now and he is there for good.

These English are everywhere! The nineteenth century is approaching its end and everything around us seems monotonous and gloomy—because the world is becoming English. However unknown and unmapped the village they reach, however hidden one might think the little river one is travelling along in some obscure corner of the Universe—one will always find an Englishman there, or a sign of English life!

Always an Englishman! And as English as when he left England, impervious to foreign civilizations, oblivious to religion, customs, different culinary skills, not changing one iota, not departing in one little detail from the British prototype. Stiff, erect, craggy, like their own sea-shores, they go round presuming to encounter all over the earth what they left in Regent Street, and expecting roast beef and pale ale in the Petreian Desert; on a mountain top they will wear their black coats on a Sunday, in deference to the Protestant Church, and be scandalized that the natives do not do the same; they receive their *Times* or *Standard* at the farthest ends of the earth and form their opinions not on what they see or hear around them but on the article written in London; they press ever onwards, but their souls are forever facing backwards, back to civilized man; they loathe everything that is not English and think other races can only be happy if they have the institutions, the habits and manners which make them happy in their northern isle!

A strange people, for whom it is out of the question

that anyone can be moral without reading the Bible, and strong without playing cricket, and a gentleman without being English!

And it is this that makes them so detested. They never fuse, they never lose their Englishness. There are fluid races, like the French and the German who, without losing their intrinsic characters, at least outwardly adapt themselves to the civilization which currently contains them. A Frenchman in the depths of Africa will unashamedly worship the local idols, and in China will wear a pigtail. The Englishman falls on the ideas and customs of other nations like a lump of granite in the water: and there he stays, a weighty encumbrance, with his Bible, his sports and his prejudices, his etiquette and selfishness —completely unaccommodating to those among whom he lives.

That is why he remains, in the countries where he has lived for centuries, a foreigner.

Everywhere he reigns and governs all his efforts go to reducing the foreign civilizations to the same type as his Anglo-Saxon variety. It is not too bad when they are operating in the lands of the Zulus and Kaffirs, in those vast regions of the Black World where the savage and his hut can barely be distinguished from the grass and rocks, and are mere accessories of the countryside: there they are dealing only with a raw material and no earlier form of original beauty is spoilt when they transform it to make it into their own image. To dress up the unfortunate black king Cetewayo, as they have just done, like an infantry colonel, and oblige the Basuto chieftains to learn the names of the British royal family by heart—these are perhaps acts of unbridled despotism, but they do not detract from some primitive original direction or idea. For Cetewayo, who used to walk naked, a uniform, even an infantry one, is one way of dressing him; and it is a matter of indifference whether the Basutos' heads are crammed with set invocations to their idols or with the names of the princes of the House of Hanover.

But when it is a case of working upon ancient civilizations like that of India, where forms of art and customs, literatures and institutions already exist, and in which a great race has put all the originality of its genius—then the Anglo-Saxon policy is more or less equal to the sacrilegious act of pulling down a Buddhist temple, as beautiful as one of Buddha's dreams, to reconstruct it along the hideous lines of the Stock Exchange in London; or of someone going to the divine marble of the Venus de Milo and trying, with the brutal aid of hammer and chisel, to reshape it into a likeness, complete with side-boards and frock-coat, of Lord Palmerston! The expansion of the Englishman to the East, his imperial objective, would be tolerable, even to an artist's sensibility—If he would content himself with taking his textiles there, his machines, his telegraph offices, his railways, and then letting these races use this colossal material of civilization to develop along the lines of their individual inclinations and temperaments. Let them supply the holy city of Hyderabad with gasometers and illumination—but for love of God let them refrain from sticking gas lamps in their temples if this is offensive to their rites and repellent to their taste! Let India be covered with railways, for example, supplied by Northumberland industrialists and paid for by the Indians—excellent! But at least let not the villages through which they pass—villages which the English themselves describe as little paradises of peace, of simple crafts, of innocent customs, of frugality and freshness and moral beauty—let these not be transformed into the likeness of the gloomy parishes of Yorkshire, with the introduction of a policeman, a pub, a red-brick Protestant chapel, a Bible-seller, a gin-shop, a factory belching smoke, a brothel, and a work-house!

*

But let us leave this subject. It is easy to speak ill of England. One has only to open the books of its great men, from Thackeray, the artist who created the bloodiest satire out of cold rancour, to Carlyle, the philosopher who spent his entire life viciously condemning it with the turbulent rage of a prophet.

One might say of England that—contrary to generous France—her virtues minister only to her own advantage, while her vices contaminate the world.

It is to England we owe the growing selfishness that is gradually hardening our hearts—this selfishness which is particularly English and which enables three hundred people around a lake in Hyde Park, in London's most elegant quarter, to watch a poor child drown while no one could be bothered to take the cigar from his mouth and hold out a plank to him to save his life! It is to England that we owe the growing hypocrisy which is invading the world and which leads to posters appearing in London advertising plays by Sardou or Dumas, which bear the astonishing declaration: 'adapted in accordance with the just requirements of English morality'; meanwhile in the streets below these very posters, the most deplorable stream of drunks and prostitutes you ever did see flows endlessly past!

But let us leave England's stains: the list is long. I wish to allude to only one more abominable defect that she has always had but which is now developing to intolerable proportions—her astounding conceit, her loud boasting, her fantastic chest-thumping!

It is especially at this moment, since the beginning of the Egyptian war, that those who love England, as I do, suffer when they see these extravagant attitudes fit for a braggart out of some picaresque novel. The telegrams the newspapers are sending back from the war, and even more so the comments those same newspapers offer, would be pitifully grotesque if they were not hatefully impertinent. The French (who are not modest) put thirty thousand Germans out of the fight in the Battle of Gravelotte, and yet they did not make a fraction of the self-congratulatory clamour with which the English celebrated the skirmish of Ramleh, where the Egyptians lost *forty-odd* men! They seem to lack all sense of proportion. A few days ago a correspondent of the *Daily News* announced, as though it were some heroic deed worthy of record for posterity, the fact that some soldiers on the march had given a piece of bread from their combat rations to an Arab who was dying of hunger by the wayside! Was it something exceptional to find a scrap of human compassion in English breasts? No. He wanted to prove that no army in the world goes to war bringing such a fund of clemency!

Whether they are praising the physical appearance of the regiments or the perfection of their bands, or the marksmanship of their artillery or the shape of their helmets, or the brilliance of their General Staff or the excellence of their combat rations—there is always the same stupid phrase appearing in heavy type: 'the best in the world!'

If an English guard fires upon an Egyptian guard and then retreats to his trench, this action is immediately declared as being 'as noble in its heroism as it is skilful for its prudence!'

The choirs that sing the praises of General Wolseley belong to pure farce. I should like to believe he is a great man—although he has so far done nothing more than rout a poor horde of negroes armed with arrows, who were idling beside some river in Africa; but what can one think when one reads in the *World* and other papers that he is the 'greatest general of the century'? Is there not a certain Moltke? And was there not a general called Napoleon?

The best, the most important and best produced newspaper in London, the *Pall Mall Gazette*, ashamed of all this, explains with its usual skill that all this trumpetblowing is not directed towards Europe but to Egypt 'to raise the troops' morale'! Do these regiments on a campaign in the deserts of Africa, before a most formidable enemy, have time then to read the gazettes? Does every private receive a copy of the *Times* with his morning's ration? The respectable *Pall Mall* is talking utter nonsense. The troops have their generals' words to encourage and reward them. Then, surely, no praise can be too great, and when a poor devil has marched all day, hungry and thirsty, his feet bleeding, across the sand and beneath a sky which beats down on his back like fire, and returns to camp at night, lying on a stretcher with two bullets in his body—then it is not much to tell him he is the finest soldier in the world!

Is it also to 'boost the troops' morale' that the *Times* and the *Spectator* talk, with their arms akimbo and their chins thrust forward, of 'imposing England's will upon Europe'?

No: it is mere boasting.

And it is not only in the newspapers. When one enters a club or a restaurant and talks to an acquaintance over a cup of tea, the same noisy ranting starts at once: 'We'll put paid to the lot of them. We've plenty of money. There's no resisting the English strength ... And if the world tries to do anything about it, it'll get our fist in its face! ...'

England seems to have lost its good manners.

She is strong, there is no doubt about that—but she talks of her strength with the brutality of some fairground Hercules who scowls and flexes his muscles; she is also certainly rich—but she talks of her wealth with all the coarseness of a millionaire who fills his belly while he crinkles the banknotes in his pocket.

Where is England's famous self-possession, her calm dignity? John Bull has turned into Ferrabraz. What of that banal old dictum that there is no true strength without peacefulness and no real grandeur without modesty?

Brazil and Portugal

THIS WEEK THE English newspapers have concerned themselves at great length with Brazil. A correspondent of the *Times*, charged with making a definitive inspection of the American continent, has now been giving us, in lengthy, crowded articles, the result of his year's travels and studies.

The last article was devoted to Brazil. I, never having visited the Empire, naturally have no authority to appreciate these revelations (the reporter assumes the attitude of a revealer) on matters of religion, culture, produce, trade, emigration, the national character, the standard of education, the situation of the Portuguese, the dynasty, the Constitution, the republic, *et de omni re braziliensi*, and I cannot transcribe them for they occupy, vast as the *Times* is, more space than Brazil herself occupies in South American territory. This article awoke the interest and comments of the *Pall Mall Gazette* and other journals, and this started people talking with warmth and curiosity about Brazil, and with the naive admiration for its brilliant flora, and the almost alarmed awe at its vastness, that our ancestors surely felt when the good Pedro Alvares Cabral, who had set off to search for Prester John, returned with the tidings that he had glimpsed the lands of Brazil.

In order to give you England's current opinion of Brazil, I am selecting, out of all these flowery articles, the one from the *Times* and shall make observations and explanatory notes on the work of its correspondent.

The great City newspaper begins by saying that, 'the description of the vast Empire of Brazil, with which the series of letters on the American continent closed, must have overwhelmed its readers with a feeling of admiration for the splendour, etc. ...' Twenty ecstatic lines follow this of course, like a prose version of the Fourth Act of *Africana*: Vasco da Gama, his eyes moist and his heart pounding at the rapture of such prodigious blossoms, such rare singing from such rare birds ...

Then comes the classic astonishment at the vastness of the Empire: 'The mere size of such a dominion [he exclaims] in the hands of so small a fraction of humanity is in itself a sufficiently impressing fact!'

And yet this admiration of the *Times* for the gigantic is mixed with a certain familiar air of patronage, of a superior being—which is the normal attitude of England and the English press towards nations which do not have a couple of hundred battleships, a Shakespeare, a Bank of England and the institution of roast beef ... In this case of Brazil, the protective tone is suffused with kindness.

Then the article breaks out into a hymn of praise once more: 'In Brazil nature does not need man's aid in order to brim over with riches and beauty! ... Nature herself, for her own pleasure, creates luxurious parklands! And there is no wild corner that does not put the richest hothouses in Europe to shame ...' This is certainly correct:

but the *Times*, fearing lest its readers should be led to suppose that Nature in Brazil is so replete, so indigestibly full that it does not allow, that it violently refuses to receive in its sated belly one more seed—hastens to reassure them: 'But [wisely states this learned journal] although Nature does not require Man's efforts, which other less generous soils need to unfold in fruits and flowers—*it does not, nevertheless, repel them.*' This allays our fears: we can now be sure that no farmer in those distant coffee plantations, as he scatters the first seeds over the soil, his native soil, with the fructifying aid of the hoe, will run the atrocious risk of being attacked by a shower of stones or blows by a banana tree. Nor could one expect anything else from gentle, pacific Ceres.

Having begun with such flourishes and oratorical panache, the *Times* now rushes on with practical ideas. And it begins by declaring that, according to the copious account of its correspondent, 'what is surprising in South America, (if we except that strip of earth which constitutes the republic of Chile, and a few bits of the coast of the enormous Empire of Brazil), is the vastness of its resources compared with the disappointing slenderness of the results.' It would be simple to blame the scarcity of the population. The *Times*, indeed, is well aware of it, for it straightway mentions the population in the Spanish republics, but it does not find it small: what it criticises is its apathy ... The portrait it gives us of Peru, Bolivia, Equador and the like countries is black and bitter: 'These people live in a disgraceful indolence, which is not incompatible with their arrogance and greatly exaggerated vanity! It only breaks out of this apathy when in a fit of political frenzy. All the effort employed here to make Nature fertile is made by foreigners: the natives confine themselves to envying them, to detesting them because they see them taking advantage of opportunities which they themselves did not wish to stoop to use!' This is cruel: I do not know whether it is fair: but between these lines throbs all the rancour of an Englishman with disappointing Peruvian bonds. 'And if our correspondent [continues the article] clearly shows admiration for Brazil, it is not absolute but relative, in comparison with the countries which are similar in material advantages, like Peru and the Plate, but where internal discord devours and destroys all the progress which has been stimulated by foreign activity. Brazil is Portuguese and not Spanish: and this explains everything. Its European blood comes from that part of the Iberian Peninsula in which freedom is traditional and triumphant, not suppressed.' The *Times* here abandons itself, rather too freely, to the rhythmic demands of the phrase: it seems to imagine that since the Battle of Ourique, we have been travelling along a broad brilliant path of uninterrupted democracy!

It goes on: 'When Brazil broke its colonial bonds, it had no ugly memories of tyranny and rapacity to forget: nor did it have to suppress generically all the remains of an evil past.' Indeed, poor souls! Never were we anything other than kind and scrupulous proprietors towards Brazil.

We were in that dreary position towards them of an old aristocrat, a broken old bachelor, toothless and tottering, who trembles and dribbles before a buxom comely housekeeper. It was we who were really the colony: and it was with a fearfully beating heart, between a *Salve Regina* and a *Laus perenne*, that we held out our hands there for alms.

The *Times* continues: 'Although independent, Brazil has remained Portuguese in nationality and semi-European in spirit. Through the simple fact of feeling themselves Portuguese, the Brazilian people had, and retain today, the instinct of the great duty which falls to them: to extract the noblest part of their noble inheritance ... Whatever Portugal's errors may have been, it cannot be said that it has ever been content with the mere number of its possessions, without taking care to profit from them.' The *Times* grows drowsy here, like ancient Homer.

The very thing that concerns us, and pleases us, and consoles us is this simple contemplation of the number of our possessions; to put our finger on them on the map, right here and right there; to say gloatingly, *ore rotundo*, 'We have eight, we have nine; we are a colonial nation, we are a sea-faring people!' As for 'profiting from them', to use the *Times*' judicious expression, about these sordid details, nobody cares, not the administration nor Afonso de Albuquerque's descendants. But the *Times* continues: 'Portugal's colonial empire has perhaps in former days been characterized by misfortune—but hardly ever by stagnation.' *Perhaps* is a good word: with our Eastern empire as a part of our history—one of the ugliest monuments to ignominy of all time ... Let us continue.

'From the same origin whence Brazil derives its activity it also derives its respect for the opinion of Europe, a thing no less important. The vagrant in the streets of

170

Lima, in Caracas or Buenos Aires nourishes a supreme disdain for the judgements that Europe might make of its political tragi-comedies. He is aware of nothing at all save his *Castillian blood* . . . He must surely feel how inconvenient it is to be expelled from the European credit and stock-exchanges . . . But he evaluates this circumstance only for the momentary embarrassments it brings with it. The Brazilian financier is another matter—he pays as respectful attention to the moods of the stock-exchanges of Paris and London, as to the Rio de Janeiro market itself . . .'

The *Times* sees in this symptom the consideration which Brazil has for Europe's opinion.

But where the *Times* is mistaken is when it suggests that Brazil owes this beautiful quality of obeying the judgements of the civilized world to its Portuguese blood. There is no country in the universe where Europe's judgement is more scorned, I believe, than in Portugal: on this point we are like the vagrant in the streets of Caracas, that the *Times* so picturesquely presents to us: because I call disdaining the opinion of Europe, not doing anything to deserve its respect. The opinion anyone beyond Badajoz has of us is not favourable, we are aware of that—but it does not worry us! I am not speaking here of Portugal as a political state. We enjoy reasonable respect on this count. We do not bring Europe troublesome complications; we maintain within our frontiers sufficient order: our administration is correctly liberal; we satisfy our financial obligations honourably.

We are what might be called a good nation, a race of decent people. And the nation, seen from outside and at a distance, has that honest air of a peaceful provincial home, silent and white-washed, where one expects to find a prudent family, God-fearing, well-seen in the parish, and with its savings tucked away in a stocking ... Europe recognizes this: and still it regards us with a disdainful eye. Why? Because it considers us a mediocre nation: let us be frank and use the actual word—because it considers us a *stupid* race. The *Times* itself, this august oracle, has already written that Portugal was intellectually so decrepit, so stubborn, so antiquated, that it had become a country to avoid and throw stones at!

*

The *Daily Telegraph* has already discussed this problem in a leading article: whether it would be possible to measure the extent of Lusitanian ignorance! Such observations, apart from being discourteous, are certainly malicious. But the truth of the matter is that, in so intellectual and critical and scientific an epoch as ours is, one cannot win universal admiration, neither a nation nor an individual, merely by behaving oneself in the streets, dutifully paying the baker, and obeying, head bowed, the edicts of the local government. These are excellent qualities but not sufficient. More is needed; a solid cultural background is needed, a high intellectual standard, a fine education of taste, a scientific foundation and that touch of the ideal which in France, in England, in Germany, inspires in the intellectual order the triumphant march forwards; and in the nations with less creative faculties, in little Holland or little Switzerland, they produce that eminent assembly of wise institutions which are, in the social order, the realization of the superior forms of thought.

You will say that I am absurd to expect to find a Dante in every parish, and demand that Voltaires should be born with the same profusion as mushrooms. Good gracious no! I am not saying that the country should write books, or create works of art: I should be content if they merely read the books that are already written, and showed interest in the works of art that already exist. Its sterility alarms me less than its indifference. What is painful is seeing it lie in a state of marasmus without any intellectual life, alien to all new ideas, hostile to all originality, coarse and lazy, sulking in its corner with its feet stretched out to the sun, cigarette in fingers and mouth open to the flies . . . It is this that vexes me.

And the curious thing is that the country is fully aware of this mortal lethargy and of the universal discredit it attracts. In order to rouse the nation's energy on the occasion of Camoes' centenary, the cry that was used was this: Let us show the world that we are still alive! that we still have a literature!

The country felt the dire need of affirming aloud throughout Europe that a vague light still shone within its skull . . . And what did it do? It filled its verandahs with paper streamers and jubilantly beat the drum till the skin broke. And that done, it stretched out once more in the sun, covered its face with a snuff handkerchief, and resumed its eternal siesta . . . From which I conclude that Portugal, refusing to take the smallest step in the direction of the arts and sciences to merit the respect of

Europe's intelligentsia, shows, in the same way as the beggar in Caracas does, the most supreme scorn for the opinions of the civilized world. If, then, Brazil has this eminent quality of showing interest in what the cultured world says about it, this is due to its own excellent qualities and has nothing whatsoever to do with its Portuguese blood: if it felt Portuguese, what it should logically do would be turn its back upon Europe, and pull its cloak collar further up around its ears.

But to get back to the article in the *Times*, the conclusion of its first part is that 'in wealth and ability Brazil most gloriously surpasses the other peoples of South America.' The *Times*, however, still sees disheartening circumstances in Brazil: 'Twelve million men are lost in a state greater than all Europe: the public revenue, which is twelve million pounds sterling, is many millions less than that of Holland and that of Belgium: with a coastline of 4,000 miles, and 2,600 miles at its greatest width, the value of merchandise exported by Brazil is a quarter less than that of the tiny kingdom of Belgium.'

Yet the *Times* is generous enough to admit that neither the density of the population, nor its revenue, nor the sum of its exports, constitutes the happiness of its people or its moral grandeur. Switzerland, which has two million inhabitants and precisely the same two million pounds' revenue, lives in conditions of prosperity and liberty, civilization and intellect, far superior to gloomy Russia, with its eighty million pounds' revenue and its eighty million men. 'But', continues the *Times*, 'if the small population and income and trade does not place Brazil in an adverse position, it is nevertheless a proof that

174

these people lack some of the qualities that make a nation great. If the Portuguese colonizers, supported merely by the small Portuguese throne, have made of the half of the New World conceded them by Pope Alexander, more than the Spanish colonizers who gained their strength from the great nation of Spain, this proves something in favour of Portuguese blood compared with Castillian or Andalusian or Aragonese. But that the conquests made upon nature in Brazil are so insignificant and the unconquered regions so vast—shows that the defects of the Portuguese and Spanish colonies are analogous . . .'

The rest of the article is more serious and I must translate it in full: 'The Brazilian is not, like the Bolivian or Peruvian, too proud or too lazy to deign to be aware of the sources of wealth and greatness which have been so prodigiously scattered around him. No: the Brazilian has energy enough to be calculating and ambitious. His attention is caught by the fertile inland regions. He would be only too pleased to see his network of navigable rivers covered with boats and steamships. In fact, in certain of the most thriving districts on the coast, the resident complains that an undue proportion of the public burdens weighing upon them are wasted in gigantic works undertaken on behalf of remote and savage regions, which will never, or not at least for many years, profit by them. Nevertheless, Brazil has sufficient strength in herself to offer the benefits of a wise administration to her vast territory.'

The *Times* then alludes briefly to the Brazilians' noble ambition to do everything for themselves, and their habit of viewing with annoyance important works handed over to foreign skill, preferring national scientific efforts and talent, even when these are inefficient and cost the country millions ... Then it goes on:

'But while the Brazilian is like this in political and administrative theories, anxious for Brazil to further herself, to undertake all by herself all the work necessary in her five million square miles—the Brazilian is loath to put his hand to the spade, or take the handle of the plough, which is precisely the work nature requires of him. In a continent that after three and a half centuries is still mainly virgin soil, the greatness of its republics and empires depends exclusively on manual work.

'Italians, Germans, negroes, have all been and are still being imported to do the hard work which the lords of the soil find repugnant. But, unaccustomed to the climate in certain districts, they will never be able to work as hard as the natives of the tropics. Not even in the more temperate provinces of the Empire will the immigrants ever work whole-heartedly until an example is set for them by the indigenous population, the masters of the land. The Brazilian must either work with his own hands or else give up the rich inheritance which he is too incompetent to administer. As time goes on it is becoming certain that all the vast resources of South America will become the patrimony of humanity.'

The *Times* here becomes rather confused. I prefer to explain its idea rather than translate the complicated prose; it wishes to say that the day is approaching when civilization will no longer consent to such rich lands, as in the states of South America, remaining sterile and useless, and that, if their present owners are incapable of making them realize their full value and become productive, for the benefit of mankind, then they should hand them over to stronger and more skilful hands. It is the system of expropriation for the good of mankind. A favourite theory of England's and of all rapacious nations.

The article then brutally continues: 'In Peru, in Bolivia, in Paraguay, in Equador, in Venezuela . . . in other countries too, the present occupiers of the land will gradually have to disappear and descend to that lower condition to which their character is destining them.' (Never has anything so savage been written!) 'The Brazilian people, however, have excellent qualities and England would not arrive hastily at the conclusion that it should share the unfortunate lot of its weak or stubborn neighbours . . . But considering the conditions of its land, Brazil must choose between a similar future or else work, the hard personal effort against which it has so far rebelled. If destiny had led the Brazilians to another part of the continent, a smaller and less beautiful part, they might have been allowed to dream away their existence. But the Brazilian has been granted a fifteenth part of the world's surface: this fifteenth part is, all of it, a treasure-house of beauty and riches and potential happiness; and as the responsibility is his, the Brazilian must either rise or fall completely!'

And with these words, Gambetta-wise, I finish. This letter is already longer than usual—too long for me to add a host of comments to the *Times'* article. Taken as a whole it is a favourable judgment. The *Times* being, so to speak, the printed conscience of the English middle-class, which is the richest, the strongest, the soundest of all

Europe, its authority is considerable; writing as it does about Brazil, I cannot but record its words—which must naturally be the expression of what the English middle-class thinks or is going to think for some time about Brazil, because the *Times* is the raw material with which England makes her opinions.

And, aware now that I have not always been wholly reverent towards the *Times* in these lines, I must murmur a humble *peccavi* . . .

A Children's Party

THE MOST CHARMING children's party I can remember took place in England in the country house of friends of mine, Mr and Mrs Bird, in Cornwall. It was a fancy-dress party representing, in miniature, the Court of King Arthur and his knights of the Round Table. What made this resurrection of that noble, heroic world which Tennyson made so popular, particularly interesting, is that we were in the very region of Cornwall where between banquets and battles Arthur, his Queen Guinevere and the twelve valiant knights of the Round Table lived. A short distance away from the Birds' park, on an oak-covered slope, tradition sets Arthur's Court and the marvellous and shaded city of Caerleon. The river where they fished for trout was the old Usk. It was on the Usk's cool banks that in olden days stood the monastery where, from the window of his cell, Percival's brother one night glimpsed a rose-coloured cloud pass by amid the scent of jonquils and, in the midst of it, the Holy Grail full of the blood of Our Lord Jesus Christ. And on clear days from the verandahs of the dining room, far off on the coast between the rocks, the ruins of Tintagel Castle can be discerned, which appears dark and sad beside the Cornish Sea in all the ballads about King Arthur.

The Court began to assemble early at lunch time, in the

great white drawing-room which overlooked the garden. The Birds' son, dressed as King Arthur, received his guests. The first legendary character to arrive, accompanied by his governess, was the wizard Merlin, an adorable little boy, fat and frowning, with an ivy crown, fair locks and enormous prophetic whiskers covering his pink cheeks. Then, followed by their mamas, all the other characters of that romantic chronicle began to enter, knights of five years old, armed and beplumed, plump little monks, scarcely weaned bishops with their croziers in their hands, fretful bards, minstrels dressed in silk, and fairies fairer than fairies themselves. Finally the three mystic queens of Valhalla arrived, grave little souls, the three led by the hand, covered in their black veils and escorted by a tall powdered lackey.

The drawing-room gradually became as animated as old Caerleon on a morning of a tourney. Little Master Bird, dressed as King Arthur, with his robe embroidered in gold, and ringlets of curly hair poking out from beneath the gem-incrusted crown, walked majestically between his brothers-in-arms. One lady, enchanted by the sight, wanted to give him a kiss. He repelled her brusquely, as the chaste King would have done. Only one stood prouder than he, the brave Launcelot of the Lake, who had had a little beard painted on him, and who, dressed in black armour, with a long scarlet plume waving from his helmet down to his golden spurs, never took his hand from his sword. And what seemed to increase his pride was the strip of white gauze across his cuirass, in strict accordance with the epic, made from a veil of Queen Guinevere's. She, Queen Guinevere, was the great beauty of the party—a little Irish miss with her two black plaits and eyes green as the pastures of Erin. Cool and serious, wrapped in her heavy cape of blue satin, she sat motionless in the middle of a sofa, with a smile which left a dimple in her chin, indifferent to the madrigals, insensible to the knights' exploits, her eyes forever lowered, regardless of whether the bards plucked their harps for her or her vassals fought beside the Cornish Sea.

A servant announced lunch by blowing a silver horn, as at Caerleon. And in pairs along the corridor to the dining-room the Court followed King Arthur who graciously and solemnly held the hand of the pretty Queen Guinevere. Then, though not without a certain confusion when their mothers had necessarily to be strict with the knights, the Round Table, elegant with its tableware and flowers, was filled. And nothing that the poetic chroniclers enjoined was lacking.

At the head of the table, in his chair carved by the spirits, sat the old wizard Merlin, from whom his governess had taken the prophetic whiskers so that he might eat his soup cleanly. There was no wild boar there on a golden platter, but only a modest joint of beef. But King Arthur raised his glass, tinged with a drop of Bordeaux, with all the nobility with which the other, so many centuries ago on that very same hill, had raised his goblet of mead when celebrating a victory. The dining-room, with its carved oaken roof, had the severe aspect of other eras and beyond the windows, as in the verses of the *Morte d'Arthur*, could be seen the ruins of Tintagel Castle, dark and sad beside the Cornish Sea.

The Court were as ravenous as if they had just returned

from a battle with wolves in the forests that border the Usk. Even the fairies devoured their food hungrily. Sir Galahad, the knight who had the strength of a thousand because of his immaculate purity, asked for several helpings of potato pudding, beating his fork furiously upon his silver helmet which was placed on the edge of the table, among the glasses.

Sir Bors, that radiant flower of Christian chivalry, had to have a napkin tied round his neck in order to keep his magnificent tunic of green satin clean. In the midst of all this gaiety, the hardy Percival, hampered by his armour, sat quiet and flushed as if thinking (as his namesake had done) of retiring to Wick monastery. Then suddenly and inexplicably he slid off his chair, spilling the gravy on the lap of the scheming Mordred, the most violent of all the knights of the Round Table.

Mordred behaved most unreasonably and pulled Percival's golden locks. The hero's aunt ran to his aid in alarm and then, as the famous Launcelot of the Lake was becoming turbulent, he was lifted ignominiously and screaming from the Round Table, in the arms of a servant.

After lunch, the Court of King Arthur returned to the party to enjoy themselves dancing. A delightful party! There were two extraordinary monks, in white habits, so small and unsteady that the ladies had to hold on to their arms in the quadrilles; they wanted to dance continuously, gayer than the Knights themselves, and ever ready to fling themselves into the little arms of the country girls adorned with flowers.

The pure Sir Galahad, who had by now discarded both buckler and helmet, galloped like mad with a light-footed fairy who had arrived that very morning from near Brittany, from the forests of Brocéliande. A bard, with his crown of oak leaves over his eyes, cried because he had lost his harp. There was also a prince from the North Sea, a laird from Erin and the brave Sir Bors, who had hidden themselves in a corner behind a sofa and, seated on the floor, were getting on with a merry repast of cakes when they were discovered, and they cried aloud when the ladies wished to put an end to their greediness—so unworthy of Christian Paladins.

In the corridor Mr Bird had to hold back a chubby monk who had lifted up his priestly robes and, in a fury, was about to thrash the scheming Sir Mordred. It was not possible to carry out the choicest part of the party, Sir Launcelot's courting of Guinevere. The brave Launcelot (very different from the other) seemed hard of heart and not to be charmed by ladies' smiles. He finished by having a terrible fit of sulks and fell on to his mother's lap, with two large tears hanging on his lashes and his fine scarlet plume fallen on the ground, as it might after a defeat on the field.

The babies soon began to grow tired. I myself, in the middle of the party, had had to pick up the venerable Bishop of Blackburn with his mitre and rich crozier. His soft blue eyes closed in sleep. I laid him on the sofa, beside the smallest of the Queens of Valhalla, who was already asleep there beneath her dark veil, with her fair hair loose and the lily of Paradise between her crossed hands . . .

And the holy bishop fell innocently asleep beside the mystic queen.

A Joke Played on
the *Times*

WHAT HAPPENED TO the *Times* was both lamentable and picaresque. This noble daily newspaper which inspires every sincerely patriotic Englishman with pride, and which, to the respectful eyes of the foreigner, appears as one of the solidest pillars of English society— like the very conscience of England put into print; this august journal, which never, from the day of its foundation, cited the name of a colleague, nor even lowered itself to participate in a controversy, for the same reasons of inflexible etiquette which forbade Louis XIV from arguing with Colbert; this austere gazette which would prefer to destroy its magnificent presses rather than allow them to print a *bon mot*, a jest, a humorous anecdote, or indeed any insignificant matter however charmingly put; this chaste journal which avoids the name of Zola, considering it an indecency—the *Times* in fact, the worthy *Times*, has recently been the victim of one of those pranks, as we call them, or practical jokes, as the Americans call them, which are at one and the same time wicked and ridiculous, which bring a flush of indignation to our cheeks and an unwilling smile to our lips, which make us publicly reproach the joker and secretly enjoy the farce, as if we had seen a paper streamer attached to the king's train, or an image of the Man of Sorrows with a top hat on its curly locks.

Everyone who has waded through those vast sheets of printed matter which make up a copy of the *Times*, knows that the fifth page is normally devoted to the publication of speeches made by eminent gentlemen in the world of politics, or literature, or science, or art, at meetings, rallies, banquets, inaugurations, *conversazioni*, in all those gatherings of ladies and gentlemen where England unleashes torrents of words. The *Times* is famous for these accounts. They are not summaries, nor extracts: they are the full speeches, word for word, especially taken down in shorthand for the *Times* by an experienced staff, with even the interruptions faithfully noted down, every little mutter religiously recorded, with never a 'Gentlemen!' omitted, never an 'oh' or 'ah' allowed to be forgotten—and everything is checked in detail, dwelt upon as lovingly as if it had fallen from the lips of Socrates, or from Christ preaching another Gospel.

This simple service costs the *Times* annually several thousand pounds—but it gives it the advantage of being the official record of public comment in England. All the European papers regard it as such: when a speech of Mr Gladstone is being discussed, or a lecture by Professor Huxley, or one of the Archbishop of Canterbury's sermons, there is always present, like a sacred text, the *Times'* verbatim report. An orator might deny that an adjective was incorrect, or an apostrophe too violent, when that apostrophe or adjective has appeared in brief summaries in any other newspaper: but never when it has appeared in the infallible columns of the *Times*. One is aware of the expense, the diligence, the meticulousness employed to obtain this accuracy—and this accuracy is indisputable.

When Mr Gladstone, in his electoral campaign in Scotland, launched his famous invective against the Hapsburg Empire—the courteous protest of the Austrian Ambassador was based upon quotations from the *Times*. An orator who wishes to leave a solid monument of his art and publish his speeches in volumes collects them from the infallible text of the *Times*. The *Times* is as faithful as a photographic reproduction. I am dwelling on this point in order to bring out the full horror of the jest.

Some weeks ago Sir William Harcourt, Minister of Home Affairs, made a speech in Manchester, an important speech, well-advertised beforehand and greatly looked forward to, dealing with questions which are at present troubling England—the anarchy in Ireland, the commercial treaty with France, intervention in Egypt, the creation of a Municipal Government of London, and other matters of import.

This speech, taken down by the member of the *Times*' staff in Manchester, telegraphed to their offices in London, was set up, read by the proof-readers, re-read by Sir William Harcourt's secretary, checked, confirmed, read through once more and finally, definitively, inserted into the appropriate page . . . And here is where the joke took place.

But first, to experience even greater indignation and delight, it is necessary to know Sir William Harcourt. Of all the members of Gladstone's ministry, Sir William is the most austere. His appearance is intimidating to begin with: stocky, strong-limbed, thick-set shoulders, with a commanding, pale, clean-shaven face, Sir William has the solemn, marble lines of a bust of Caesar.

And a rigid doctrinarian spirit inhabits this Roman figure: a liberal (in comparison to the Marquis of Salisbury, who is completely feudal), Sir William represents tradition, the Whig spirit in the government. He is the conservative counter-balance in this radical Ministry; he is there, like a block of constitutional granite, to prevent the other ministers, like Chamberlain, Sir Charles Dilke, the disciples of Stuart Mill, from progressing too far along the broad path of Revolution; and that is why he has this heavy solemnity of manners, this pomposity of expression, like one who feels it is his honour to guard the highest things—the Crown, the Church, the aristocracy, the privileges and integrity of the Empire . . . He is a solemn fellow. Even when he is buttoned up in his jacket he looks as if he is wrapped in a toga. He is a morose man, dull, incapable of smiling, and has that air of official majesty which reminds one of both Guizot and an elephant.

And when one watches him in Parliament, grave, severe, dressed in black, it is impossible to imagine him in any informal attitude, seated on a sofa smoking a cigarette, with one leg crossed over the other, let alone on his knees, with a lady's hand clasped in his, murmuring sweet nothings.

It is this which makes the prank so atrocious and so delightful . . . This solemn statesman's solemn speech was set up then, ready to go to press, when *someone*, taking advantage of a moment in which the security staff of the *Times*' offices relaxed their vigilance for a instant, *someone*, a monster, a felon, subtly, stealthily made his way to that speech, tore out ten or a dozen lines and substituted others for it, composed beforehand, and most treacherously and skilfully composed! And what lines they were! Good Lord! How can I, without sullying myself, possibly explain the words to the readers of the *Gazeta de Notícias*?

These lines, interpolated in the grave minister's grave speech, were (I shudder to say this) erotic ones! They were a convulsive cry of inordinate lewdness, they were the noise of a beast excited by all the furies of Venus; they were like the hoarse, dry call of the stag in the woods on a quiet midsummer day; they were the drunken stammerings of the Fauns of mythology, of the God Priapus, of the goat-men, the satyrs who wandered over the sacred slopes of Mount Olympus, howling, crushing the white lilies, violating the hearts of the roses, flinging themselves about with the ferocious leaps of billy-goats as they glimpsed, between the branches of the elms, the fair nymphs of the waters . . . It was all this, and more.

And a further nicety of the jest was that this did not sound discordant, it did not jar upon the senses, coming suddenly and out of context, like a dunghill set amid the rosy blooms of rhetoric. No: it had been fitted in with devilish skill. Sir William Harcourt was accusing the Conservatives of affecting a patriotic melancholy in the presence of the supposed dangers, which, under the liberal regime, beset the great principles of the monarchic order, the very integrity of England. And here he asked them, most naturally in a natural flight of oratory: 'Why these groans? Why this exaggeration of public sorrow? Certainly the questions of Ireland and Egypt are grave:

but Her Majesty's government knows that glorious and advantageous solutions will not be long in coming . . . We are calm. I, for my part, feel the tranquil certainty of one who, after fulfilling an official duty, is rewarded with the serene and approving smile of his conscience, etc., etc.'

And it was precisely at this point that the mischievous lines made a natural appearance, developing further this affirmation of intimate contentment, showing the exuberant spirit of a merry-making minister who, satisfied with the glorious state of public affairs, suggests that the nation's delight should take the most justifiable eccentric form—of a tremendous orgy, of some gigantic spree . . . Sir William continued (let it be understood that I am using only approximate and attenuated expressions; to translate word for word what appeared in the *Times* would be to destroy the reputation of the *Gazeta de Notícias* for ever . . .) Sir William went on: 'I, for my part, am happy. I feel like going on a spree! Why should we not, indeed, have a real feast, with rivers of wine and willing women? Ah—lovely wenches! You ladies who are listening to me now, let down your hair and let's have some merry-making, let's have an orgy! Here's to our debauch! Bring on the champagne! Here's to love; let's have some rapture! . . .' This is just to give you the idea: what was written in the *Times* was expressed far more crudely, in far more orgiastic terms!

Now imagine the effect the following day, when thousands of numbers of the *Times*, containing this abomination, penetrated those reserved English homes, where (so they say) the worthier type of Christian family lives. The *Times*, the most expensive of newspapers, is the beloved paper of the aristocracy, of the upper bourgeoisie, of high finance. One cannot imagine an English gentleman, the classical English gentleman, who does not straightway in the morning conscientiously digest his *Times*: it is like the very heart of England, which he holds for a moment in his hands and in which he proudly witnesses every day an increase of strength, a great pulsating vitality. Normally it is at breakfast that one reads the *Times*: and that morning, seeing on the fourth page the headlines about 'Sir William Harcourt's Speech in Manchester', he would naturally peruse it with interest, both because of its national importance and because of the affection he feels for Sir William, for his historic name, his pure, upright principles, his high position . . .

Imagine the scenes! Here an old and devout duchess, full of enthusiasm about social questions, settles herself in her fine tapestry armchair in order to savour fully Sir William's noble oratory. Suddenly she stops abruptly, stares at the *Times*, wipes her spectacles, imagining she has not read correctly, then turns back to the paper and reads again, passes a trembling hand over her face, searches anxiously for her smelling salts, turns once more to confirm whether she has not been the victim of a hallucination and finally, flinging aside the filthy journal, leaves the room with offended steps, thinking that these, then, are the results of a century of democracy, of materialism and licentiousness!

Nearby a couple of newly-weds, ensconced on the same sofa beside the fire, their arms entwined, read the *Times*, not so much to learn about the question of Egypt, as to read the *compte-rendu* of other elegant weddings or the

news from Paris, where they intend to finish their honey-
moon; but they come upon Sir William's speech and are
glancing through it vaguely when suddenly the filthy
stream of erotic apostrophising flows out from the page!

In another house there is a fair fresh creature of
eighteen summers, a pure domestic lily, who reads out the
Times to an old uncle of hers, a gout-ridden general, a
revered relic of the Peninsular wars; the old man listens,
little interested by the politics of the day, which he
detests, but very attentive to the charm of that golden
voice at his side; suddenly, however, the poor angel
stammers, stops, turns a rose-like hue, trembles, and
shame brings tears to her eye. She flees, and leaves the
vile *Times* in the hands of the astonished general. Or else,
worse still, the sweet young thing, with the innocence of a
hot-house flower, does not understand, imagines that *this
is politics*, and reads on in her voice of gold—and suddenly
her worthy uncle hears issuing from the rose-bud lips,
made to murmur only the chastest sounds of Weber, a
filthy torrent of lewdness.

It's frightful! And what is curious about the incident
is that this dastardly trick was discovered in the *Times'*
offices only at 11 o'clock the following morning: that is,
when the newspaper had already been distributed in
London, and carried off by the early morning trains to the
provinces and by the Dover ferry to all Europe! The
Times' administration telegraphed to all their agents
throughout the world to withhold distribution and buy *at
any price* the shameful copies already sold.

These telegrams alone cost nearly two *contos*. But the
best of it is that as soon as the story of the catastrophe

leaked out, and it was known that the *Times* was buying the wretched edition at any price—this edition immediately became an object of value, a security, a source of speculation, with a value in the market equal to, if not higher than, the bonds issued by many a civilized nation. I know of a restaurant which had a regular order for four copies of the *Times*—and which sold its blighted copies for two pounds each.

Greater profits than that were made however. The *Times* did not haggle over the price it paid. And it is said that it has so far spent nearly forty *contos* buying back this ill-fated edition.

The author of the jest has not yet been discovered. He is undoubtedly a monster, and seriously deserves the heavy sentence that would prove his ruin if he were found and brought before any English court. But on the other hand, considering that forty *contos* is merely a minimal amount of the *Times'* great fortune, and that this austere journal carries its pedantry and its haughty *pruderie* so far as to condemn as obscene the very mention of the works of Zola and other realists—I cannot help but think, with a certain glee, that Providence is armed with strange and terrible weapons!

Never, surely since printing was invented, has a newspaper published on its choicest page, in large print, twelve filthy lines of the most shocking obscenity; and that it should be the *Times*, the most important, the most humourless, the most solemn, most pedantic, most revered of all papers that have existed since printing began—is, let anyone say otherwise, highly amusing.

And to conclude, let me invite charitable and honest souls to have a good laugh at the *Times'* expense.